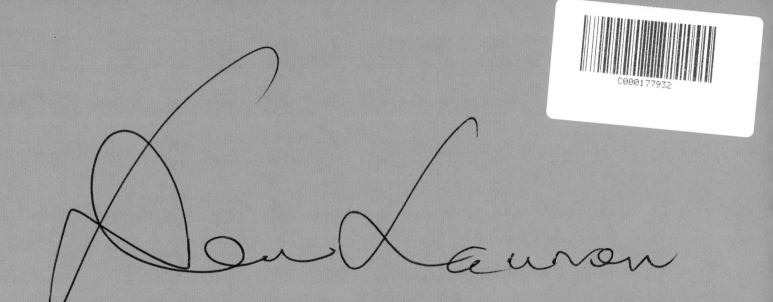

JAPANESE COOKING AT HOME
Hideo Dekura

First published in Australia in 2005 by
New Holland Publishers (Australia) Pty Ltd
Sydney • Auckland • London • Cape Town

14 Aquatic Drive Frenchs Forest NSW 2086 Australia
218 Lake Road Northcote Auckland New Zealand
86 Edgeware Road London W2 2EA United Kingdom
80 McKenzie Street Cape Town 8001 South Africa

National Library of Australia Cataloguing-in-Publication Data:

Japanese cooking at home.

Includes index.
ISBN 1 74110 260 X.

1. Cookery, Japanese. I. Title.

641.5952

Publisher: Fiona Schultz
Project Editors: Jacqueline Blanchard, Lliane Clarke
Designer: Joanne Buckley and Karl Roper
Production Manager: Linda Bottari
Printed in China by C&C Offset Printing Co.,LTD.

ACKNOWLEDGEMENTS

In completing this book, I have received much support and encouragement from my family, my extended family and friends, producers and distributors, and many people who are involved in Japanese food.

One of my best friends, Mrs Jill Elias has assisted greatly, guiding me over the hurdles of English.

Dr Ngyuen and his wife showed me around their beautiful farm and generously offered their fresh vegetables with such wonderful earthy aromas. I am grateful to such hard-working producers who make it possible for me to be able to cook authentic Japanese dishes.

Special thanks to my kitchen assistant, Ms. Keiko Kobayashi.

Also, without Keiko Yoshida and the editorial team at New Holland this book would not have been possible.

Special thanks to
Blue Stripe Australia, for supplying the beef
Hakubaku Australia, for supplying Japanese noodles
House Foods Corporation Japan, for supplying wasabi
Japan Food Cooperation, for supplying varieties of Japanese ingredients
Kikkoman Australia, for supplying soy sauce products
Kirin Brewery Co. Ltd Australia, for supplying Kirin-Beer
Mitsukan Japan, for supplying Mitsukan products
Nagai Food Co. Pty., for supplying nori sheets
Sunbeam Australia, for supplying kitchen appliances
Sunmasamune Australia, for supplying Goshu-sake
Sydney Fish Market Authority, for supplying fresh fish and seafood
Wheel and Barrol Australia, for supplying kitchenware

CONTENTS

INTRODUCTION

One of the fundamental teachings of the Buddhist faith is that impermanence and change are integral to the very nature of existence. A thing of beauty is a joy, but not necessarily a joy forever. A single cherry blossom will not last for long, yet it is eagerly anticipated, enjoyed while it blooms, and remembered nostalgically when it has long faded. If one blossom should fall in our glass while we are drinking under the cherry blossom trees in the park in spring, we consider ourselves to be lucky. Japanese people embrace change enthusiastically, yet still we have the need to make the moments last, to hang on to the precious times.

Somehow, I see food in much the same light. The excitement of preparing a meal, the pleasure of tasting the flavours and the warmth of companionship are momentary, yet linger in the memory long after the dishes are washed and stored away.

Some of my earliest memories relate to food. In a family of eight children, every meal was a major event. In post-war Tokyo there was no gas, so all the food was cooked on a simple wood burner. Because my father was a restaurateur, we had a supply of ingredients envied by the local community, although he never cooked at home. Meal preparation was very much a case of all hands on deck. My particular job was to rise early and buy the tofu and natto from the street vendors.

I was about twelve before we got our first gas cooker and I still wonder at how my mother managed to produce daily pots of rice and miso and all those other delights from that wood oven, without the convenience of gas or an electric rice cooker. Her concern for nutrition and avoiding waste, and her love of the fresh daikon, soy beans and potatoes growing in the vegetable garden out the back were probably all motivating factors in my choice to pursue cooking as a career.

Lunches provided at school after the end of World War II were American style but because the flavours were so different they were not at all popular. I soon came to learn that this was all we would get, and because food was so scarce I should take advantage of it. Apart from the regulation school milk, I soon learnt to eat and enjoy Western-style food, although my great delight was to be able to take a homemade o-bento of o-nigiri, a large rice ball enclosing a pickled plum, with an apple and a few sweets as a treat when we went on a school excursion.

Although our meals were very nutritious, with lots of rice, noodles, miso, tofu, vegetables and fish, vegetable oil was not available, so the dishes we had in the evening, such as fried fish, stir-fried vegetables or korokke were all cooked with lard, as was my favourite afternoon snack of fried sweet potato, sprinkled with black sugar and sesame seeds.

Festive occasions hold special memories for me. I can still see us gathered together, washing and chopping cabbage, layering it with rice bran, chilli, kombu and salt in large barrels to make the hakusai pickles in preparation for New Year celebrations. We were supposed to wait until New Year's Day, but I could never resist digging in to the barrels with my fingers. The delicious red bean mixture encasing a ball of sweet sticky rice held the same temptation for me. Three days of food preparation beforehand meant that from New Year's Day there would be no cooking in the house for three days, a welcome break for my mother, and a custom which households all over Japan still enjoy today.

Cooking methods have changed over the years, and many new foods and cooking styles have been introduced to Japan. Even old favourites, such as tempura, pork cutlets and mabō-dōfu, which my mother frequently cooked for us, had their origins in other countries. New ingredients have crept into old recipes, and foreign dishes are regularly cooked, often with a Japanese touch. Most families succumb to fast foods and instant food at times, but home cooking is still enjoyed everywhere. Traditional Japanese cooking remains so dear to the heart (or the stomach) that, even when Japanese people travel, they often seek out the old familiar dishes, and can't bear to go for too long without a bowl of short grain rice.

As a working single father, I was always pressed for time, and one of my major concerns was how I could provide nutritious meals for my son when I had a limited time to spend preparing and cooking meals at home. At that time, I would ask myself how my mother managed to cook tasty and nutritious meals for our big family with such limited resources. Recalling and recreating those dishes made me appreciate the true value of simple family cooking, not only to satisfy the appetite, but also to feed the soul.

I was inspired to write this book when I realised that many people I talk to about Japanese cuisine tell me that they love Japanese food, but have never tried cooking it because they think it would be too difficult, or they are not familiar with the ingredients. In writing this book, I wanted to share with you some of the simple home delights, which may seem exotic to you, but were part of my now-treasured everyday experiences growing up in Japan.

I hope you will discover just how easy it is to cook Japanese food at home for your family and friends. Before eating we say 'itadakimas', which means I gratefully receive, and on finishing we say, 'gochisō-sama deshita', in other words 'that was indeed a feast, thank you'.

Hideo Dekura

JAPANESE MEALS

A typical Japanese meal consists of rice, soup, a main dish and two or more side dishes. The dishes are served in individual small bowls or on plates, and eaten with chopsticks. Soup is served with all the other dishes rather than preceding the meal, as is the case in Western-style dining. Traditionally a meal at home is not divided into entrée and main. Desserts are sometimes served, but more commonly fruit is eaten after a meal. It is usually cut up by the mother at the table. Green tea is drunk any time throughout the meal, but of course alcoholic drinks such as beer, sake and wine are also drunk if desired.

LUNCH BOXES

Lunch, as well as other meals, usually consists of rice along with small portions of tasty, cooked morsels. When lunch is taken from home, it is conveniently carried in a small box and is known as o-bento.

The desire for people to have such conveniently portable and attractively displayed lunches has led to a thriving industry in Japan. Of course, some mothers still prepare o-bento for their families, but an endless variety of o-bentō can be purchased relatively cheaply from almost any store where food is handled.

Department stores, supermarkets, convenience stores, railway stations, small kiosks and shopping malls all sell a huge selection of lunch boxes with flavours to suit all tastes and budgets. You can even order o-bento from a choice of set menus in restaurants. The boxes are usually divided into small compartments, so the rice is kept separate from the other ingredients, which include a selection of cooked foods and pickles.

ENTERTAINING

When guests are invited for a formal meal at home it is customary to serve each person an array of small dishes on individual trays. This display of food on attractive chinaware can look quite spectacular, particularly to a Westerner who is unaccustomed to this style of dining. Eating at low tables, sitting or kneeling on cushions is still the custom, though many homes have Western-style tables and chairs too. At a casual party, dishes are served in large bowls and plates so guests can serve themselves.

Japan is a country where the seasons are usually clearly defined, and there is a great respect for nature, so meals have tended to be planned on a seasonal basis using fish, vegetables and even floral decorations relating to the particular time of the year. However, more recently, as imported foods become readily available, this tradition is seeing many changes. As well as seasonal foods becoming available all year round, foods from other countries are also available, and it is not uncommon for party buffets to provide a variety of international dishes.

PANTRY LIST

Here are my suggestions for the basic Japanese ingredients to include in your pantry. You can expand the list of foodstuffs as you go.

Dried shiitake: A strong, distinctively flavoured mushroom, good for making dashi-stock.

Furikake: Pre-prepared mixture of various seasoned condiments which can be sprinkled on top of dishes, included in rice or used as an outer coating.

Goma/Sesame seeds: Available in black and white. Used as flavouring and condiment.

Harusame/Spring rain noodles: Fine potato starch noodles. Used in hot pots or decoratively when deep-fried, as they puff up and become white.

Katsuo Bushi/Bonito flakes: Dried, smoked, mould-cured bonito flakes. Used as a flavouring and a garnish.

Kome/Short grain rice: Japanese rice is also called Japonica rice. It is a short, wide-grain rice with a starchy texture when cooked.

Kombu/Dried kelp: This is essential for making dashi-stock.

Katakuriko/Japanese potato starch: Used for thickening and for coating foods before dipping in tempura batter.

Katakuriko/Potato starch

Harusame/Spring rain noodles

Furikake/Seasoned condiments

Mirin/Cooking rice wine

Kumbu/Dried kelp

Shoyu/Soy sauce

Mirin/Cooking rice wine: Made from sticky rice. It has a subtle sweetness which enhances the flavour of the ingredients during cooking.

Miso: Fermented paste of soy beans. Miso is used for soup, and as a seasoning in sauces and dressings.

Nori sheets: Roasted seaweed sheets, for wrapping sushi rice, and for seasoning garnishes.

Seasoned Nori strips: Small pieces of seasoned seaweed.

Sake/Rice wine: Adds a refined touch to some dishes, and will reduce the fishy smell when cooking fish.

Nori sheets/Roasted seaweed

Shichimi/Japanese seven-spice: Seven-spice chilli mix. Serve as a condiment with hot noodles and hot pots.

Sesame oil: A few drops enhances the flavour of many dishes.

Shoyu/Soy sauce: Common soy sauce is indispensable in Japanese cooking. A salt-reduced, as well as light colour and Tamari varieties, are also available.

Su/Rice vinegar: Vinegar which is made from rice. It has a rice flavour and sourness to suit Japanese cooking.

Tamari: Common soy sauce but richer and thicker. Suitable for sashimi.

Miso/Soybean paste

Noodles

Usukuchi-Shoyu/Light colour soy sauce: This soy sauce is saltier than common soy sauce, but lighter in colour.

Wasabi paste: Japanese green mustard. Available in paste and powder form, the paste variety being the hotter. A little goes a long way.

Kome/Short grain rice

Su/Rice vinegar

Wasabi paste/
Green mustard

JAPANESE ALCOHOLIC DRINKS

SAKE

Sake is Japanese rice wine, produced from fermented cooked rice. It is produced throughout Japan by big companies and small local breweries, known as jizake. Sake is also now being produced in countries outside Japan.

There are many varieties, due to differing manufacturing methods, and the regional differences of water and rice. The flavour ranges from dry to fruity and fairly sweet. The alcoholic content is in the range of 13% to 15%; some sakes can have an alcoholic content as high as 50%, so be careful.

Traditionally, sake is served in small cups or glasses, cold or at room temperature in summer, and warmed slightly in winter. It is usually served with a meal, or with a salty snack.

SHŌCHŪ

Shōchū is distilled spirits, made mainly from sweet potato. It may be drunk 'on the rocks' but is normally mixed with water, soda water or with various flavoured syrups in a cocktail. It is available from licensed Japanese grocery shops.

UME-SHU

Ume-shu is a liqueur made of shōchū or sake with Japanese plums and rock sugar. In summer, it is drunk to recover from heat exhaustion, and in winter it is good for a sore throat. It is available from licensed Japanese and Asian grocery shops.

JAPANESE BEER

Beer has been produced in Japan since it was introduced at the beginning of the twentieth century, and is drunk throughout Japan, particularly in summer. There are now a number of well-known beer companies in Japan, such as Kirin, Sapporo and Asahi which are fast gaining popularity throughout the Western world as well.

EQUIPMENT AND UTENSILS

For the photos in this book I used plates and bowls from local shops and I imagine you too will be able to easily find suitable plates in your kitchen for serving and eating Japanese food. You do not need to rush out and buy any special kitchenware.

However, if you feel like treating yourself, here is a list of some useful utensils. All are available from specialised Japanese stores. If you are lucky enough to go to Japan, you could purchase some there as special souvenirs.

Han-giri/Sushi rice bowl: A large, shallow, wooden bowl for mixing sushi vinegar mixture and cooked rice. As a substitute, you can use a wooden salad bowl or shallow bowl.

Japanese tweezers: Tweezers with flat tips that hold fish bones firmly and enable easy bone removal. They are available from local knife shops.

Japanese grater: A fine grater of tin-coated copper, stainless steel, ceramic, aluminium or even plastic is useful for grating daikon radish, ginger or garlic.

Sashimi knife: This long, thin-bladed knife is designed for slicing fish for sashimi and sushi as well as preparing other food. Like a Samurai sword, this Japanese knife is sharpened on one side of the blade only, which results in very effective cutting. However, special care must be paid to sharpening, which should be done regularly using a water stone.

Slicer or grater: Any slicer or grater is useful, but a slicer with detachable blades is more versatile to use.

Sudare or Maki-Su/Sushi roll bamboo mat: Bamboo mat for rolling sushi.

Suri-Bachi and Suri-Kogi/Japanese grinding bowl and wooden pestle: Designed for crushing and grinding materials such as sesame seeds. The inside of the mortar has a ridged pattern. The pestle is wooden. Many sizes are available. To use, place a cloth under the bowl, rotate the pestle and press down to crush the materials using the tip of the pestle.

Vegetable cutters: A great gadget for creating fun shapes. Seasonal images such as flowers or autumn leaves are most popular.

Rice

Rice is the staple food for the Japanese. Japanese rice is of the Japonica type, a short, wide-grain rice which has a starchy texture when cooked. Properly cooked rice tends to be slightly sticky with the grains clumping together, but it should never be mushy.

Because of the great variety of rice available in Japan, choosing the best rice is always a hot topic in Japanese households around harvest time. Outside of Japan, there is limited choice of short grain rice, but the following few tips will help you to cook rice in a way which suits Japanese dishes.

- Rinse raw rice thoroughly.
- Drain for at least 30 minutes.
- Steam rice for 20–30 minutes after cooking.
- Add mirin or honey for extra flavour (½ teaspoon per 1 cup of uncooked rice).

PREPARING RICE

4 cups short grain rice
4 cups water
extra water

1. Using the measuring cup provided with rice cooker, place 4 cups of rice into a bowl that holds twice the volume of rice.
2. Pour water into bowl until it just covers the rice. Holding the bowl with one hand, stir rice briskly for 10–15 seconds with the other hand (photo 1).
3. Carefully tip the milky water out, covering rice with one hand (photo 2).
4. At the second and third rinse, add ample water and stir again for about 30 seconds to remove excess starch. Tip out water.
5. Run cold water over rice for about 1–2 minutes, until water becomes clear.
6. Transfer rice to a fine-mesh sieve to drain and leave for 30 minutes (photo 3).
7. Place rice and measured water into the rice cooker pan. Wipe the underneath of the pan with a dry towel and set it into the rice cooker. Switch on.
8. When cooked, leave for 20 minutes to steam.
9. Before serving, turn rice over gently with a moistened rice paddle to allow excess moisture to escape as steam.

- *When rinsing, do not soak the rice for any length of time, as water will be absorbed.*
- *When you have left-over rice, keep it in the freezer, wrapped with plastic wrap or in an airtight container. Sandwich bags with a zipper are quite convenient.*

Rice Balls O-nigiri
おにぎり

The Japanese equivalent to a sandwich, 'o-nigiri' are one of the most popular items for a picnic, school lunch or as a fast food item in convenience stores. The addition of salt helps to preserve them. They are clumps of rice encasing a filling shaped into a triangle or oval, and many are wrapped in a strip of nori for easy handling. They are eaten at room temperature. The size varies, ranging from a triangle of about 10x10x10cm to much smaller sizes. A triangle measuring about 6 cm is a good size to serve at informal gatherings.

100g (4oz) salmon fillet, grilled and flaked
salt
4 cups hot, cooked, short grain rice
green peas rice (page 22) or
mushroom rice (page 22)
furikake (salted, roasted, sesame seeds
or in many other varieties available
from Japanese grocery shops)
roasted nori strips

a bowl of salted water
(2 cups water mixed with 1 tablespoon salt)
for finger dipping
(The water keeps the rice
from sticking to your hands
while the salt helps preserve
the rice balls.)

1. Prepare the salmon filling and season to taste with the salt.
2. With moistened paddle place rice into a bowl.
3. Wet hands with salty water.
4. Transfer a ball of rice about the size of a baseball into the palm of your hand.
5. Place some filling into the middle of the rice by first making a hollow with your finger.
6. Using both hands, mould the rice into a triangular shape. Press the rice only just hard enough to keep the rice firmly together.
7. Set the rice triangles down on a plate and sprinkle lightly with one of the varieties of furikake.
8. A strip of nori can be wrapped around the edge or across the surface of the triangle.

- *Other fillings can be tuna with mayonnaise, Japanese pickled plum (umeboshi), bonito flakes with soy sauce, cooked vegetables or pickles.*
- *If you do not like soggy nori, wrap the nori just before eating. However, the o-nigiri hold together best when nori is wrapped around warm rice.*
- *When grilling o-nigiri, mould firmly. Or place o-nigiri in a plastic bag and flatten like hash brown potatoes. Serve with soy sauce and butter.*

Green Peas Rice Mame-gohan
豆ごはん

Makes approx. 4 cups cooked rice

2 cups short grain rice
1 cup fresh or frozen green peas
2 cups water
1 tablespoon mirin
a pinch of salt

1. Rinse rice and place in the rice cooker. Cover with a layer of the green peas. Add water.
2. Sprinkle mirin and salt over rice.
3. Cook and steam as per basic cooking rice (page 18).

- *You can substitute corn kernels (fresh or frozen) for peas.*

Mushroom Rice Kinoko-gohan
きのこごはん

Makes approx. 4 cups cooked rice

2 cups short grain rice
2 cups super dashi (page 66)
1 tablespoon sake
1 tablespoon light colour soy sauce
4 fresh shiitake mushrooms,
or dried shiitake soaked in water until soft
1 packet enoki mushrooms, bases discarded
4 oyster mushrooms

1. See preparation of rice (page 18). Place rice in the rice cooker.
2. Add super dashi, sake, soy sauce and mushrooms.
3. Cook and allow to stand in covered rice cooker for a further 20 minutes.

- *Other ingredients such as chopped carrot, corn kernels, sliced daikon or slices of fried bean curd (abura age) can be added to the rice.*

Fried Rice Yaki-meshi

焼きめし

4 cups cooked left-over rice
½ cup fresh or frozen green peas,
cooked and drained
½ cup fresh or frozen corn,
cooked and drained
2 eggs
vegetable oil
1 garlic clove, crushed
1 small carrot, peeled and chopped
1 spring onion, chopped
1 teaspoon salt
a pinch of pepper

1. Warm rice briefly in microwave. Cook peas and corn separately and drain well.
2. Break eggs into a bowl and stir.
3. Heat a pan over high heat, add a small amount of oil. Add egg mixture to pan, stirring constantly. Transfer scrambled egg onto a plate.
4. Add more oil to pan, add garlic, carrot and spring onion and stir for 1 minute with wooden spoon.
5. Add green peas and corn, then warmed rice stirring continuously. Add scrambled egg.
6. Sprinkle with salt and pepper and stir-fry for a minute.

- *If you prefer a curry taste, add 1 tablespoon curry powder.*
- *For Tokyo-style fried rice, add soy sauce instead of salt.*
- *Other ingredients such as chopped ham, bacon, cooked chicken thigh or roasted duck may be added.*

Chicken and Egg with Rice Oyako-don

Serves 2

親子丼

Oyako means 'parent and child' because both chicken and egg are used in this dish. Don comes from the word Domburi, a 'large bowl' in which savoury rice or hot noodles with soup are served.

150g [5oz] chicken breast fillet
1 tablespoon mirin (cooking rice wine)

DASHI MIXTURE
3 tablespoons light colour soy sauce
1 tablespoon caster sugar
1 tablespoon sake
70 ml [3fl oz] super dashi (page 66)

a few drops vegetable oil
1 brown onion, sliced
1 stem spring onion,
sliced diagonally
2 eggs, beaten
2 bowls cooked rice

1. Cut the chicken into bite-sized pieces and marinate with mirin.
2. To make dashi mixture, heat soy sauce, caster sugar, sake and super dashi in a saucepan, then set aside. (This can be done in a microwave oven in about 1 minute.)
3. Pour a little of oil in a frying pan and stir-fry chicken until cooked through.
4. Add onion and stir until lightly brown. Then add spring onion and stir another minute.
5. Add the dashi mixture and bring to the boil, then reduce heat.
6. Pour beaten eggs in a circular motion over the simmering mixture. Set over low heat until the egg is just cooked.
7. Place a portion of hot rice into each bowl and slide half of the chicken and egg toppings over the rice in each bowl.

• *You can top with tempura (page 110) or pork cutlet (page 114).*

Beef Rice Gyūdon

Serves 2

牛丼

SAUCE
½ cup super dashi (page 66)
4 tablespoons soy sauce
1 tablespoon caster sugar
1 tablespoon mirin
1 x 2cm [¾in] fresh ginger, grated

vegetable oil
1 small brown onion, sliced
200g [7oz] thinly sliced rump steak
½ spring onion stem, chopped
2 bowls cooked rice, kept warm
1 tablespoon red ginger pickles

1. To prepare sauce, place all sauce ingredients in a saucepan and simmer for 3 minutes, occasionally stirring.
2. Heat a small amount of oil in a frying pan.
3. Add onion and beef, stirring until lightly brown.
4. Add spring onion and stir for a few seconds, then add the sauce and simmer for 3 minutes. If scum forms on the surface, remove with a spoon.
5. Place warm rice in individual bowls and pour the beef mixture over it.
6. Top with red ginger pickles.

• *Udon noodles can be used instead of rice.*

Tempura on Rice Tendon

Serves 2 (pictured right)

天丼

6 tempura king prawns or tempura
of your choice (page 110)

SAUCE
⅔ cup super dashi (page 66)
1 tablespoon soy sauce
1 tablespoon mirin
1 teaspoon caster sugar

2 bowls cooked rice, warmed

1. Prepare tempura.
2. Combine all the ingredients for sauce in a saucepan and bring to the boil over a high heat. Simmer over low heat for 3 minutes.
3. Place warm rice in each bowl, top with tempura, then pour over the sauce.

Rice in Omelette Omu-raisu

Serves 2

オムライス

3 eggs
salt
cracked black pepper
vegetable oil
100g [4oz] chicken breast fillet,
cut into 0.5cm [⅓in] cubes
½ small onion, peeled and chopped
4 tablespoons fresh or frozen green peas, cooked
4 tablespoons fresh or frozen corn kernels, cooked
4 mushrooms, cleaned and stems discarded
2 cups cooked rice, warmed
tomato sauce
a few sprigs of parsley

1. Beat eggs in bowl with a pinch of salt and pepper.
2. Heat up the frying pan and oil lightly.
3. Pour in ¼ beaten egg and cook until the surface becomes dry.
4. Transfer to a plate and make 3 more omelettes.
5. Wipe pan with kitchen paper and add some more oil. Add chicken and onion and stir-fry until cooked.
6. Add green peas, corn and mushrooms; season with salt and pepper to taste while stirring.
7. Add warmed rice to the pan and stir with a wooden spatula, combining rice with other ingredients.
8. Lay an omelette on an individual plate and place half of the rice mixture on one half. Fold over the other half of the omelette.
9. Drizzle tomato sauce decoratively over the omelette. Garnish with parsley sprigs.

Sushi

SUGGESTED INGREDIENTS

For fillings try extra fresh fish such as salmon or tuna; smoked salmon; canned tuna mixed with mayonnaise; tempura; vegetables such as steamed asparagus or wilted English spinach; carrot sticks (or julienne of carrot) blanched in some boiling water to which a little sugar has been added; fresh salad leaves; avocado; fresh tomato; cheese or ham.

SUGGESTIONS FOR SAUCE

Soy sauce and wasabi are a basic combination. However, tamari (soy sauce without wheat) goes well with sashimi. If you like to have less salt on your food, choose salt-reduced soy sauce, or combine with super dashi to reduce saltiness. Or be innovative with sweet chilli sauce or a mixture of olive oil and soy sauce mixture.

PRESENTATION

Depending on the occasion, sushi can be served in many different ways. It makes a perfect first course for Western-style dining, when it can be served on individual plates. For a large gathering it can be attractively displayed on large platters. Be imaginative with your decorations and garnishes.

Preparing Sushi Rice

4 cups rice, cooked

SUSHI VINEGAR MIXTURE
1 cup rice vinegar
3½ tablespoons caster sugar
a pinch salt

Equipment you will need:
• a wooden sushi bowl (or wooden salad bowl)
• a rice paddle (or a wooden spatula)
• hand fan or electric fan
(or a piece of cardboard)
• muslin cloth or kitchen towel

1. Wipe the inside of the wooden bowl with a damp cloth to moisten. Transfer cooked rice from rice cooker into the centre of the sushi bowl.
2. Prepare the sushi vinegar mixture by combining all ingredients in a bowl.
3. Gradually pour sushi vinegar over slicing paddle across the bowl to break up lumps. Mix rice evenly around the bowl with a slicing action. While mixing, cool the rice with a hand fan. This helps rice absorb vinegar mixture and creates a glossy surface on rice.
4. When rice becomes lukewarm, cover with a damp muslin cloth.

• *Keep rice at room temperature. Do not refrigerate, as this dries out the sushi rice and causes the starch to break down.*
• *To colour sushi rice, use beetroot juice or black (coloured) rice for natural colour.*

PREPARING SUSHI ROLLS
Slender Roll Hoso-maki
細巻き

Makes 6 pieces.

This is the basic method for rolling up sushi. Once you master this, try large rolls and inside-out rolls.

1 nori sheet, halved crossways
1 cup sushi rice (page 32)
wasabi paste
¼ Lebanese cucumber, cut lengthwise,
 seeded and cut into long thin sticks
salt-reduced soy sauce
pickled ginger, optional

Use Te-zu (vinegar water) for handling rice,
made by combining 1 cup of water
with 1 teaspoon rice vinegar.

 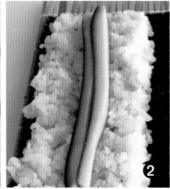  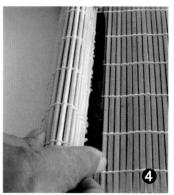

ROLLING METHOD [right-handed]
1. Place bamboo mat on a board or other dry flat surface.
2. Place half a sheet of nori on the mat, rough side up, one edge of the nori lining up with the front edge of the mat.
3. Dip your right fingers into the vinegar water. With damp fingers, take sushi rice and spread evenly over
   ⅔ of the nori, leaving a space at the back edge. With your right index finger, draw a line of wasabi along the rice
   (photo 1).
4. Place strips of cucumber side by side along the wasabi line (photo 2).
5. Using both hands, lift the front edge of the mat and roll up to the end of the rice. While still wrapped, gently shape
   the roll, pushing rice in at both ends with fingertips (photo 3).
6. Keep lifting up front edge of the bamboo mat as you roll the sushi on to the remaining uncovered portion of nori,
   giving a final light press on the edge before removing the mat completely (photo 4).
7. With a wet knife, slice the roll in half, then into thirds.
8. Serve with pickled ginger garnish and a dipping dish of soy sauce.

* *Spread rice with wet fingers, but do not splash nori.*
* *For your first attempts at making sushi, keep fillings to a minimum for ease of rolling.*
* *For more variety, you can make more sushi using other suitable fillings such as cooked carrot sticks and asparagus.*

34 sushi

Large Roll Futo-maki

Makes 8 pieces

太巻き

Futo-maki (literally 'fat roll') is a larger roll made using a whole nori sheet, a larger amount of rice and 3 to 6 fillings.

1 sheet nori
1½ cups sushi rice (see page 32)
wasabi paste
¼ Lebanese cucumber, cut lengthwise,
seeded and cut into long thin sticks
¼ carrot, cut into lengthwise strips and cooked with
a small amount of sugar for 5 minutes
1 Japanese omelette (see page 84), cut into strips
¼ grilled eel (Available in a vacuum-sealed packets
from Japanese grocery shops. Cut off one strip
about 1cm wide along the length of the eel.)
soy sauce or salt-reduced soy sauce
pickled ginger, optional

Te-zu (vinegar water) for handling rice
(see page 34)

Place the nori on the bamboo mat, and proceed as for the method for the slender roll (page 34).

• *A great variety of fillings can be used for these rolls, enabling you to vary the colours and textures. However, avoid fillings which are juicy, such as unseeded tomato. Suggested fillings are avocado, asparagus, green salad leaves and cooked poultry, beef or pork.*

Inside-out Roll Hadaka-maki
はだか巻き

Makes 8 pieces

1 sheet nori
1½ cups sushi rice (page 32)
wasabi paste
1 tablespoon Japanese mayonnaise
2 green salad leaves such as baby cos lettuce
2 large king prawns, cooked, peeled and deveined
2 stems of asparagus, cooked, lower portion removed
roasted white sesame seeds for decoration

Te-zu (vinegar water) for handling rice (see page 34)
a sheet of plastic wrap

1. Place nori on the bamboo mat. With wet fingers spread rice all over the nori (photo 1).
2. Spread a piece of plastic wrap over the rice.
3. Place one hand on top of the plastic wrap, one hand underneath the mat and gently turn up side down. Remove the mat and place it underneath. The resulting arrangement is now the bamboo mat on the bottom, then the plastic wrap, rice and nori on top. With your finger, draw a thin line of wasabi and mayonnaise along the nori. Place salad leaves along the centre of the nori. Place the prawns and asparagus along the central area of the salad leaves (photo 2).
4. Using both hands (dry), roll up about two thirds of the way (photo 3).
5. Lift the mat and pull free the edge of the plastic wrap so it doesn't get caught in the roll. Roll the last bit, and remove the mat but not the plastic (photo 4).
6. With a sharp wet knife, cut in half and then quarters, making 8 pieces. Remove the plastic wrap. Decorate with roasted sesame seeds.

• *Other ingredients suitable for topping are roasted black sesame seeds, tobikko (flying fish roe) and egg mimosa (made by passing the yolk of a hardboiled egg through a sieve).*

Hand-wrapped Sushi Roll Temaki-zushi

手巻き寿司

This is a great dish for informal occasions or summer Sunday lunches. Everyone can sit around the table and make their own sushi from a platter of pre-prepared ingredients.

4 cups sushi rice (page 32)
4 sheets of nori, cut into quarters
wasabi paste
Japanese mayonnaise

ANY SELECTION OF THE FOLLOWING FILLINGS:
4 fresh salmon slices, sushi-sliced (page 52)
½ Lebanese cucumber, sliced in quarters, seeded and cut lengthwise into thin sticks
4 small green salad leaves
½ avocado, peeled and sliced
100g [4oz] can of tuna, mixed with 1 tablespoon Japanese mayonnaise
¼ carrot, peeled and cut into thin strips
4 asparagus, cooked, lower section cut off
2 shiso leaves
processed cheese, cut into thin sticks
100g [4oz] grilled eel, sliced

salmon caviar, optional
reduced-salt soy sauce

1. Prepare all the ingredients on a plate and put rice in a bowl.
2. In your left hand hold a sheet of nori and with a wet spoon put sushi rice in the centre.
3. Add a little wasabi and mayonnaise to taste. Place on top any combination of the fillings.
4. With your right hand wrap up the nori, making a cone shape.
5. Spoon caviar on top.
6. Serve with soy sauce.

• *Many other ingredients can be included on the platter such as ham strips, tempura, grilled chicken or beef strips, prawns or smoked salmon.*

Hand-ball Sushi Temari-zushi
手まり寿司

Makes 5

Kids love this bite-sized sushi. It is a good choice for an o-bento lunch box.

1 egg, beaten with 1 teaspoon mirin and
a pinch salt
vegetable oil
1 cuttlefish
1 king prawn, cooked, peeled,
deveined and butterflied
1 slice smoked salmon
1 small slice proscuitto
2 cups sushi rice (page 32)
wasabi paste
soy sauce

5 sheets of plastic wrap, about 10cm

1. To make thin egg omelette, heat a non-stick frying pan over moderate heat. Pour in a little vegetable oil. Lower heat, pour egg mixture into pan and tilt quickly to spread evenly over the bottom. When the surface of the egg is almost dry, use a spatula to loosen edges and then insert spatula under and carefully flip the omelette. Cook for 10 seconds more and remove from pan onto a dry board. Cut into 2cm-wide ribbons.
2. To prepare cuttlefish, discard bone, peel the skin off with fingers, and rinse. Blanch in boiling water. With a knife, open and slice as for sushi topping (see page 52).
3. Lay a sheet of plastic wrap on a board and place an ingredient, such as king prawn, cut side up on the centre.
4. Top with an amount of rice about the size of a golf ball. Draw edges of plastic wrap over rice and prawn, while twisting together and shape into a ball.
5. Repeat with other ingredients.
6. Just before serving, remove plastic wrap and decorate with a small amount of wasabi and nori threads.
7. Serve with soy sauce.

Hand-moulded Sushi Nigiri-zushi
握り寿司

_right>*Makes 22 pieces,
sufficient for 2 main meal servings*

2 cups sushi rice (including rice in cucumber roll)
2 green king prawns
(see instructions, right)
2 slices salmon sushi
2 slices tuna sushi
2 slices cuttlefish (see Temari-zushi on page 42)
2 slices king fish sushi
1 stuffed green olive, cut in half
2 stems of snow pea sprout
2 snow peas, blanched
wasabi paste
4 pieces cucumber sushi roll (page 34)
2 slices of egg omelette (page 84),
pickled ginger for garnish
soy sauce

Te-zu (vinegar water) for handling rice
(see page 34)

TO PREPARE GREEN KING PRAWNS
green king prawns
bamboo skewers
1 cup rice vinegar
½ cup water
2 tablespoons caster sugar

1. Rinse prawns. To keep prawns from curling during par-boiling, pierce with skewers along the belly side from head to tail.
2. Bring water to boil in a saucepan and add a pinch of salt. Simmer prawns for 3 minutes over moderate heat, then plunge into cold water.
3. Remove skewers. Remove shells from prawns, but leave tails intact. Devein.
4. Make a slit on the belly side to open up like a butterfly. Then gently flatten out.
5. Combine vinegar, water, sugar and place prawns in this mixture until ready to use.

  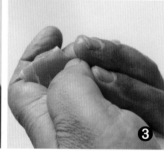 

NIGIRI TECHNIQUE METHOD
1. Have the sliced and other ingredients ready. Place a dry board on the kitchen bench.
2. Moisten hand with the vinegar water and pick up about 1 tablespoonful rice. Form into a ball, pressing gently with the hand but do not squash. Pick up a sushi slice with your other hand and spread on a dab of wasabi with one finger of the hand holding the rice (photo 1).
3. Place rice on the sushi slice and with index and middle fingers press firmly to form a mounded shape (photo 2).
4. Roll sushi over and press again with two fingers against the fish (photo 3).
5. Rotate sushi 180° and press again with two fingers against the fish (photo 4).
6. Arrange on a platter with sushi rolls and slices of omelette. Garnish with pickled ginger; serve with soy sauce.

Tofu-pouch Sushi Inari-zushi
いなり寿司

Makes 6 pieces

This is popular for picnic lunches, particularly served in combination with other sushi such as cucumber rolls.

tofu (bean curd) pouches (abura-gea), available from Asian grocery stores
2 dried shiitake mushrooms, soaked in water for at least 15 minutes and chopped finely
¼ small carrot, peeled and chopped finely
1 cup super dashi (page 66)
½ cup soy sauce
2 tablespoons mirin
1 tablespoon caster sugar
3 cups sushi rice (page 18)
cucumber roll to accompany (page 34)
soy sauce

saucepan lid or saucer or sheet of foil smaller than size of saucepan to be used

PREPARATION OF BEAN CURD POUCHES
To remove the excess oil from the bean pouches, place the pouches in boiling water and leave for a minute, then drain and squeeze out the water and unwanted oil.

1. Place bean curd pouches, shiitake mushrooms and carrot in a saucepan. Add dashi, soy sauce, mirin and caster sugar. To keep bean curd submerged while cooking, place a smaller lid or saucer on top. Bring the mixture to the boil and simmer over low heat for about 10 minutes. Remove from heat and allow to stand until liquid is cool.
2. Remove bean curds and squeeze to remove excess water. Transfer to cutting board and cut each in half to make two pouches. Set aside.
3. Mix the shiitake and carrots into sushi rice with a rice paddle.
4. Carefully open the bean curd pouch. With wet fingers, make a small ball of rice and place it into the pouch. Press sides with fingers to make a pillow shape. Tuck ends of pouch inside. Repeat with the other pouches.
5. Arrange on a platter with cucumber roll. Serve with soy sauce.

- *Present these sushi in o-bento box with cucumber rolls and a small container of soy sauce.*
- *Roasted black sesame seeds can be sprinkled over the rice before tucking in the flap of the tofu pouch.*
- *Seasoned, pre-cooked bean curd pouches are available from Japanese or Asian grocery shops.*
- *Leave some pouches open to vary presentation.*

Scattered Sushi Chirashi-zushi

Serves 2

ちらし寿司

This is a dish for celebrating the change of season, and for happy occasions. Typically sushi rice is mixed with various ingredients, then topped with seasonal vegetables, fish or egg. Other traditional ingredients are seasoned kampyo strips, shredded thin omelette, snow peas and grilled eel. More recently, corn, blueberries, or even tempura may be added for extra colour. It may be served in a large bowl, individual bowls or even a box.

¼ daikon radish, sliced
½ cup rice vinegar
¼ cup water
1 teaspoon caster sugar
2 dried shiitake, soaked in water at least 15 minutes
1 cup super dashi (page 66)
1 tablespoon caster sugar
1 tablespoon soy sauce
1 tablespoon mirin
2 stems Chinese broccoli
4 green king prawns, heads removed, deveined and rinsed
2 cups cooked sushi rice (page 32)
2 hard-boiled egg yolks, sieved (egg mimosa)
½ cup fresh or frozen green peas, cooked
4 tablespoons salmon caviar
wasabi paste
soy sauce

1. To make pickled daikon flowers, cut daikon slices with a flower-shaped cutter. Soak slices in a mixture of ½ cup rice vinegar, ¼ cup water and 1 teaspoon caster sugar mixture for 30 minutes.
2. To prepare shiitake, discard the stems and slice. Put dashi-stock, caster sugar, soy sauce and mirin in a saucepan; add shiitake slices. Simmer for 10 to 15 minutes over low heat.
3. Blanch Chinese broccoli for 1 minute and drain. Cook king prawns in salted water for 2 minutes, then drain.
4. Squeeze shiitake mushrooms to remove excess liquid and mix with sushi rice. Place sushi rice into individual bowls or one large bowl.
5. Sprinkle egg mimosa and green peas over the top. Decorate with broccoli, king prawn and salmon caviar set on pickled daikon flower.
6. Serve with wasabi and soy sauce.

- *Left-over daikon can be used in agedashi-dofu (page 96) or pot cooking (page 134) as garnish.*

DIPPING SAUCES
Dipping sauces are available at Asian groceries, but they are easy to make if you wish to make your own (see page 142). They can be made well ahead and stored in airtight containers in the refrigerator for a couple of days.

Sashimi

Many fishmongers are now well aware of the requirements of fish for sashimi, but if you have any doubts, keep in mind the following:

• The colour of fish fillets and cut pieces should be bright and the surface neither dry nor slimy.
• With whole fish, the eyes should be bright not smoky. Behind the gills should be bright not pale. The flesh should feel plump.

Remember all fish should have a fresh ocean smell. When you are buying fish, it is a good idea to take along a cool box and ice to preserve the freshness on the way home. Store covered in the refrigerator and if possible eat the same day.

Filleting and slicing techniques for sashimi and sushi toppings

If you are a novice at filleting fish, start with smaller fish such as trevally, then progress to larger fish like snapper, which has bigger bones. Snapper needs some practice, however, it is worth a try because its flesh has more flavour and it is delicious as sashimi.

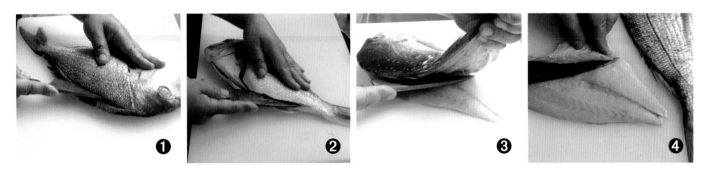

1. For filleting a fish with large scales, such as kingfish, first remove the scales using a scaler in a plastic bag. The skin under the scales is edible.
2. Position the fish flat on a board with the tail closest to you, head away from you, and the back fin on your right. Hold the fish with your left hand. Insert the knife at the point just behind the head bone, with the tip of the blade pointing slightly toward the fish head. Move the knife toward the tail, slicing the blade along the backbone (photo 1).
3. Change the position of the fish so the head is pointing toward you and the tail fin is on your right side. Holding the body with your left hand, insert the tip of the knife into the belly side from the tail and slide the knife in moving along the backbone toward the head (photo 2).
4. Turn the fish over. To separate the fillet from the bone, insert the tip of knife at the tail end. Holding up the tail, move the knife along the backbone to the head. Push the blade of knife down and cut fillet off (photo 3) .
5. Trim off the remaining bones on the fillet. Repeat with the other side of the fish to make another fillet (photo 4).

Cut slices of salmon fillet with
the grain to make pieces
6cm long, 2.5cm wide and
0.3cm thick. You can use
left-over pieces of fish for
salads or scattered sushi
(page 50-51).

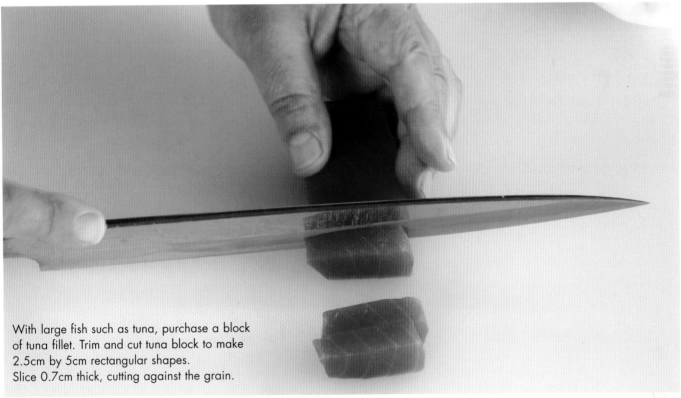

With large fish such as tuna, purchase a block
of tuna fillet. Trim and cut tuna block to make
2.5cm by 5cm rectangular shapes.
Slice 0.7cm thick, cutting against the grain.

Basic Sashimi Sashimi
さしみ

This simple dish of tuna sashimi is served on a bed of fine daikon strips which can be dipped in soy and eaten along with the tuna.

a block of tuna fillet, approx. 300g [11oz]
¼ daikon radish, peeled
wasabi paste
tamari or salt-reduced soy sauce

PREPARATION OF DAIKON
Traditionally the daikon garnish is prepared by peeling it off in a continuous sheet.

Start by peeling and cutting out a 10cm cylinder of fresh daikon. Holding the daikon in one hand, place the edge of the knife vertically on the daikon and cut in a sawing motion to peel a continuous sheet.

Carefully roll up the sheet, and cut into thin julienne. Soak in iced water until ready to use.

This may be rather difficult for novices. Try using a vegetable peeler or Japanese-style slicer (available from Japanese, Chinese or Korean shops) or a mandolin to slice off thin daikon strips. Then roll up and cut into thin julienne as before.

1. Slice tuna.
2. Arrange daikon garnish and top with sliced tuna.
   Serve with wasabi and salt-reduced soy sauce.

Japanese-style Beef Carpaccio Beef-Tataki

Serves 4

ビーフタタキ

RICE VINEGAR MIXTURE
½ cup rice vinegar
1 tablespoon caster sugar
a pinch of salt

¼ brown onion, thinly sliced and soaked in water
400g [14oz] beef sirloin or rump steak (in one piece)

DRESSING
1 tablespoon light colour soy sauce
1 teaspoon grape seed oil or extra virgin olive oil
1 tablespoon rice vinegar
1 clove garlic, grated (or chopped
fresh chilli if you prefer)
1 very small knob fresh ginger, grated
1 teaspoon sake
1 teaspoon caster sugar

shiso leaves or any green salad leaves
1 cherry tomato, quartered

wasabi paste (optional)

sake or plum sake (ume-shu)

1. Combine all the ingredients for rice vinegar mixture in a bowl.
2. Drain onion and place in the mixture.
3. Heat up a frying pan over a high heat. Cook the beef until all surfaces turn light brown. Transfer into iced water for 3 seconds. Drain and pat dry with kitchen paper.
4. Place beef in the vinegar mixture and refrigerate for 20–30 minutes.
5. Meanwhile, mix all dressing ingredients in a bowl and set aside.
6. Remove the beef from the vinegar mixture and transfer to a chopping board. Slice beef thinly with a sharp knife.
7. Arrange salad leaves and slices of beef on a plate. Add onion slices and garnish with pieces tomato. Drizzle dressing over the meat; serve with wasabi if desired.
8. Accompany with plum sake or sake.

• *This dish can be made using bonito or tuna instead of beef.*

Sashimi Salad Sashimi sarada
さしみサラダ

Serves 2

1 raw sashimi-quality snapper fillet
baby green salad leaves
1 tomato, sliced
1 spring onion, chopped
1 teaspoon capers

DRESSING
1 tablespoon rice vinegar
1 teaspoon caster sugar
1 tablespoon olive oil
1 tablespoon soy sauce

lemon wedges
1 stem common mint

1. Slice snapper fillet into sashimi (page 52)
2. Arrange green salad leaves and tomato on a plate.
3. Place sashimi snapper slices in centre.
4. Top with spring onion and capers.
5. Make dressing by combining all ingredients in a bowl and sprinkle over salad and sashimi.
6. Serve with the lemon wedges and mint leaves placed off to the side.

• *This dish makes a nice accompaniment to both Japanese and Western dishes.*

Marinated Salmon Sāmon-no sujime

サーモンの酢じめ

A sashimi dish such as this may look quite exotic to a non-Japanese person, but it is really very simple and can be prepared very quickly at home and dressed down or up according to the occasion.

3 salmon sashimi slices
(page 52)
¼ brown onion, thinly sliced
and soaked in water

VINEGAR MIXTURE
½ cup rice vinegar
1 tablespoon caster sugar
a pinch of salt

6 small sticks of fresh ginger, cut as
very fine julienne
1 stem common mint

1. Prepare salmon sashimi slices.
2. Drain onion well.
3. Combine all the ingredients for the vinegar mixture in a bowl.
4. Marinate salmon slices with onion slices in vinegar mixture for 30 minutes.
5. Transfer onion slices to a plate and top with salmon slices and criss-crossed ginger sticks. Arrange sprigs of mint on top of the ginger sticks.

Soup

Traditionally, Japanese soup is made with the stock from dried shiitake and products from the ocean such as dried kelp, bonito flakes and anchovies. It has no fat, but there is flavour from the natural 'Umami' glutaminic acid in the stock.

'Miso' or 'miso soup' is made from a paste of fermented soy beans and grain, usually either barley or rice, with salt added. It has a distinctive taste and aroma, and is used as a flavouring in soups and dressings.

In the home, soup is usually served with every meal, including breakfast. Included in this chapter are recipes for basic dashi (stock) and also super dashi (see page 66) which can be used in many soups, stews and sauces.

Japanese Stock

The following three stock recipes comprise some of the main ingredients used in this book. They are all simple to prepare.

Kombu (dried kelp)

Kelp has glutaminic acid that enhances the flavours in food. It is a great natural resource, containing minerals from the ocean, which dissolve in water.

After purchasing, cut into pieces and keep in an airtight container ready to use any time. Before using, wipe with a cloth. Korean or Chinese dried kelp may be used as a substitute; Japanese kelp is thicker and firmer, but the taste is similar.

Overnight kombu dashi (dried kelp stock)

2 x 5cm [1¾in] square pieces of dried kelp, wiped with a dry cloth
500ml [¾pt] water

Add kelp to water, then simply keep in a jar overnight for breakfast soup or prepare in the morning for dinner. In summer, refrigerate kelp in water overnight and in winter keep at room temperature. Remove kelp before using the stock.

Cooked kombu dashi (kelp stock)

2 x 5cm [1¾in] pieces of dried kelp, wiped with a dry cloth
500ml [¾pt] water

Soak kelp with water for at least 15 minutes in a saucepan, then slowly bring to the boil with the lid on. Remove from the heat and set aside for 10 minutes. Discard the kelp.

Shiitake (dried shiitake mushroom)

These mushrooms have a strong flavour which complements other ingredients. You will find they go well with Western dishes too. Before using, rinse and soak in water until softened (about 15 minutes). They are also available sliced.

Overnight shiitake dashi (shiitake stock)

3 dried shiitake mushrooms, rinsed
500ml [¾pt] water

Prepare in the same way as overnight kelp dashi. This is a strongly flavoured stock.

Cooked shiitake dashi (shiitake stock)

3 dried-shiitake mushrooms, soaked
at least 15 minutes
500ml [¾pt] water

Place shiitake with water in a saucepan and heat with a lid on over moderate heat until boiling. Simmer over low heat until reduced by half to give a more concentrated flavour.

Katsuo-bushi (dried bonito flakes)

Dried bonito has a dry-roasted fish aroma. Packaged bonito flakes are available from Japanese and Asian grocery shops. As a topping, serve over tofu, yaki-soba noodles or Japanese savoury pancake. Soaked in soy sauce, bonito flakes can also be used as a filling in rice balls.

Super dashi Bannō-dashi

Makes approx. 1 litre

This is the best and most versatile dashi for soups, stews and sauces.

500ml cooked kelp dashi
500ml cooked shiitake dashi
20g dried bonito flakes

1. Combine kelp dashi and shiitake dashi in a saucepan and bring to the boil over a moderate heat.
2. Add bonito flakes, turn the heat to low and simmer for 1 minute.
3. Turn off the heat and when the bonito flakes have sunk, sieve the stock with a fine strainer or a sieve lined with muslin or cheesecloth.

This stock can be stored in a sealed bottle in the refrigerator for 2 days or in the freezer for 1 month.

- *Instant powder or liquid stock can be purchased from Japanese and Asian grocery stores. However, although convenient, commercially prepared stocks are rarely as tasty as the homemade variety.*

Clear Soup Osumashi おすまし

Serves 4 (pictured right)

This soup has a gentle taste, cleansing your palate between dishes. It is good with delicately flavoured dishes, such as sashimi or sushi.

16 o-fu (decoratively shaped, compressed gluten patties used as a garnish and available from Japanese grocery shops)
4 cups super dashi (see above)
a few pinches of salt
½ tablespoon sake (or mirin)
1 teaspoon light soy sauce
4 mitsuba leaves (or watercress)

1. Soak o-fu in water according to the instructions on the packet.
2. Bring super dashi to boil in a saucepan.
3. Season with salt, sake and soy sauce.
4. Add mitsuba and o-fu before serving.

- *Other clear soups can be made by using snapper stock instead of dashi.*
- *The addition of a small amount of ginger juice will enhance the flavour of clear soups.*

Miso Soup Miso-shiru

味噌汁

There are many varieties of miso available in Japan, but outside Japan the most frequently found varieties are red miso, brown miso and white miso. Brown miso has a well-balanced flavour and aroma; red miso has a stronger flavour; white miso is sweeter and less salty.

Miso soup is served in homes, restaurants and cafeterias daily throughout Japan. It is a valuable source of protein in the Japanese diet.

4 cups super dashi (page 66)
2 tablespoons light brown miso paste, mixed well with 1 tablespoon mirin
¼ small packet silken tofu, cubed
1 pinch of dried wakame-seaweed, soaked in water
1 spring onion stem, chopped

1. Bring super dashi to boil in a saucepan.
2. Add miso and dissolve over low heat.
3. Add tofu and wakame and simmer for a couple of minutes.
4. Pour the soup into individual bowls.
5. Sprinkle spring onion over the top.

• *Other ingredients such as sliced abura-age (deep fried tofu), pumpkin, potato, carrot, beans, shiitake mushrooms or zucchini can be added.*

Pork Soup Ton-jiru
豚汁

Serves 4

Mainly root vegetables are used in this warming soup.

200g [7oz] pork fillets, thinly sliced
⅓ carrot, peeled and sliced
100g [4oz] fresh or frozen
gobo (burdock)
100g [4oz] pumpkin, cut in narrow
wedges and trimmed
100g [4oz] daikon,
peeled and sliced
4 cups shiitake dashi and the shiitake
mushrooms from the dashi, sliced
(page 66)
1 clove garlic, crushed
vegetable oil
2 tablespoons light brown miso,
mixed with 2 tablespoons sake
1 small amount fresh ginger,
finely sliced
1 spring onion stem
shichimi (Japanese seven-spice)

1. Prepare the pork, vegetables and garlic. If you can get fresh burdock, clean and cut it diagonally. Leave in water until ready to use.
2. Drop a little vegetable oil in a saucepan heat, add pork and and stir for 1 minute.
3. Add carrot, burdock, pumpkin, daikon, shiitake and shiitake dashi, garlic and super dashi while stirring.
4. Simmer for 30 minutes over low heat.
5. Add miso and ginger and cook for another minute.
6. Serve in individual bowls, topped with spring onion. Sprinkle shichimi (Japanese seven-spice) over the soup.

• *Other ingredients which can be included in this soup are sweet potato, potato and konnyaku (Japanese yam potato).*

Noodles

Like Italian pasta, there are many varieties of Japanese noodles. They are available dried or fresh. Dried noodles are easy to stock in your pantry. Fresh noodles such as udon or soba are sold frozen or vacuum-sealed packs. In hot weather, you can enjoy cold noodles with a dipping sauce and in cold weather hot noodles with soup makes you warm and cozy.

COMMON NOODLES

Egg noodles: Although originally Chinese these thin noodles are popular in Japan, either as 'instant noodles', or in simple home cooked dishes. These noodles are eaten in soup (ramen) or stir-fried (yaki-soba). There are specialised noodles for ramen and yaki-soba. In summer, cold egg noodles with sauce of vinegar mixed with caster sugar, soy sauce and sesame oil.

Harusame (potato starch noodles): Literally means 'spring rain' noodles. Similar to Chinese thin rice noodles (glass noodles), but the Japanese ones are made from potato starch. Use in hot pot dishes.

Udon (thick wheat noodles): Available vacuumed packed, frozen and dried. Fresh udon noodles are delightfully tender but, strong.

Soba (buck wheat noodles): Dried soba is easy to find even in local supermarkets.

Somen (thin wheat noodles): Usually served cold as a refreshing summer dish. Boil following the package directions and rinse in cold water. Serve with dipping sauce with garnish, such as chopped spring onion.

Hot Udon and Soba Noodles in Soup
Udon and Soba うどんと蕎麦

Serves 2

1 bundle of udon
6 cups super dashi (page 66)
2 tablespoons light colour soy sauce
1 tablespoon mirin
salt
vegetable tempura of your choice
(page 110)
shichimi (Japanese seven-spice)
1 bundle of soba
1 spring onion, chopped

1. Bring a large pan of water to the boil and cook udon according to the directions on the packet, then drain.
2. Meanwhile, heat up the super dashi and add soy, mirin and salt.
3. Place udon noodles in a bowl with half the soup.
4. Top with tempura and sprinkle with shichimi.
5. Similarly, cook soba and pour in the remaining soup.
6. Top soba with chopped spring onion.

- *For the topping, blanched English spinach, deep-fried tofu (page 96), cooked carrot slices or fresh enoki, shimeji or shiitake mushrooms can be used.*
- *If using dried shiitake mushrooms for the topping, prepare by rinsing the dried shiitake and soaking in water for at least 15 minutes. Add 1 teaspoon soy sauce, 1 tablespoon caster sugar and a pinch of salt. Bring to the boil and simmer for 15 minutes. Allow to stand for 30 minutes.*

Cold Udon and Soba Noodles Buffet-style
Hiyashi-udon and Soba 冷やしうどんと蕎麦

Serves 4

DIPPING SAUCE
4 cups super dashi (page 66)
2 tablespoons soy sauce
2 tablespoons mirin
a pinch of salt

1 bundle dried udon, cooked
(page 74)
1 bundle dried soba, cooked
(page 74)

ACCOMPANIMENTS
4 Japanese shiso leaves or your
choice of herbs, cut in strips
4 tempura of your choice
(page 110)
1 ripe tomato, unseeded
and chopped
1 spring onion stem
1 Lebanese cucumber, chopped
1 tablespoon grated daikon radish
1 tablespoon grated fresh ginger
1 tablespoon dried wakame,
soaked in water and drained
1 teaspoon shichimi
(Japanese seven-spice)
wasabi paste

ice cubes

1. To make dipping sauce, put all the ingredients for the sauce in a saucepan and bring to boil. Remove from the heat. Cool in refrigerator until ready to use.
2. Cook udon and soba noodles, drain and cool.
3. Prepare accompaniments and set on plates.
4. Place ice cubes in 2 large bowls, top with udon in one bowl, soba in the other.
5. Eat from individual small bowls with accompaniments and dipping sauce.

Udon and Soba Noodle Salad
Udonan Soba Sarada うどんと蕎麦のサラダ

Serves 2

DRESSING
⅓ cup super dashi (page 66)
1 teaspoon mirin
1 tablespoon soy sauce
1 teaspoon caster sugar
2 tablespoons rice vinegar
1 tablespoon macadamia nut oil or peanut oil

TOPPINGS
2 Italian basil leaves or shiso leaves
1 slice proscuitto or other ham, cut into bite-sized pieces
2 tomato wedges
small amount of parmesan cheese, shaved

½ bundle dried udon
½ bundle dried soba

1. Prepare dressing by placing first four dressing ingredients in a saucepan; bring to the boil. Allow to cool. Store in a bottle with a lid in refrigerator until ready to use. Before using, add rice vinegar and macadamia nut oil.
2. Prepare toppings.
3. Cook noodles separately in boiling water (page 74).
4. Rinse under running water. Drain well.
5. Place noodles in bowls and arrange toppings.
6. Serve dressing on the side in a small jug.

Yaki-soba Stir-fry Yaki-soba

焼きそば

Serves 2

300g [10½oz] yaki-soba noodles
vegetable oil
1 garlic clove, chopped
100g [4oz] sliced pork fillet
2 cabbage leaves, cut
into small pieces
½ carrot, peeled and sliced
2 fresh or dried shiitake mushrooms
1 spring onion, sliced diagonally
salt
white pepper

YAKI-SOBA SAUCE
2 tablespoons tomato sauce
2 tablespoons Worcestershire sauce
1 tablespoon super dashi
(page 66)
1 tablespoon soy sauce
1 tablespoon honey

red pickled ginger
aonori (green nori flakes)
or bonito flakes

1. Cook noodles and drain well.
2. Put oil in a pan and heat. Add garlic, sliced pork, cabbage, carrot, shiitake and spring onion, stirring all the while.
3. Season to taste with salt and pepper.
4. Make sauce by combining all ingredients together.
5. Add noodles and sauce to pan while still stirring.
6. Place the noodles onto individual plates and top with red picked ginger, green nori or bonito flakes.

- *Yaki-soba is a very versatile dish. You can add almost any vegetable from your fridge, such as mushrooms, onion, capsicum or asparagus as well as seafood or chicken.*
- *Instead of egg noodles, you can use udon noodles.*
- *You can cook yaki-soba on the barbecue.*
- *Commercially prepared yaki-soba sauce is available from Japanese or Asian groceries.*

Egg

Egg is a very common ingredient in many countries and can be served in a variety of ways. Being available throughout the year, it is a convenient quick-fix meal. Here are some ideas and recipes to add to your repertoire.

Japanese-style Omelette Tamago-yaki

玉子焼き

Serves 2

4 eggs
2 tablespoons super dashi
(page 66)
1 tablespoon caster sugar
1 tablespoon mirin
1 teaspoon light colour soy sauce
1 tablespoon vegetable oil

1 tablespoon grated daikon
radish or red radish
soy sauce

1. Crack eggs into a bowl and add super dashi, caster sugar, mirin and soy sauce then whisk.
2. Strain into another bowl.
3. Place a non-stick frying pan over a medium heat for 1 minute. Pour in a little oil and swirl evenly over the pan.
4. Pour in one third of the egg mixture and cook until set around the edges.
5. With a spatula fold one third towards the front of the pan, then fold over again in the same direction onto the remaining portion.
6. Add a little more oil to the pan and pour half of the remaining egg mixture onto the empty area of the pan and cook until the edge sets.
7. Again fold one third towards the folded egg, then fold this over on top of previous roll, making a flat roll on one side of the pan.
8. Add more oil and pour in the remaining egg mixture, and repeat the folding process. With the spatula, give a little push to mould the shape.
9. When cooked, remove from the heat, and place on a bamboo mat on a dry surface. Wrap the omelette with the bamboo mat and shape. By pressing with your fingers on one side only along the length of the roll, you can make a wedge shape which produces attractive 'petals' when cut across the roll. It can also be left as a cylinder or squared off.
10. Cut into pieces. Serve with grated daikon and soy sauce.

玉
子

Steamed Savoury Egg Chawan-mushi

Serves 2

茶碗蒸し

This delicious dish has a quite runny consistency, unlike many Western 'custard-style' dishes which are generally firmer.

2 eggs, beaten
1½ cups super dashi
(page 66)
1 tablespoon light colour soy sauce
1 teaspoon mirin

1 small fresh shiitake mushroom,
(dried shiitake mushroom
soaked in water) sliced
2 cubes of chicken breast
fillet, uncooked
2 small green king prawns,
peeled and deveined
2 mitsuba or snow pea sprouts

2 pieces foil for lids

1. Bring water in a steamer to the boil, then reduce heat to simmer.
2. Meanwhile, prepare egg mixture by combining all ingredients together in a bowl.
3. Strain egg mixture and pour into 2 cups.
4. Add shiitake, chicken and king prawns to egg mixture.
5. Cover each cup with a piece of foil. Carefully place them into the steamer. Steam over low heat for approx. 10 minutes. To check if cooked, insert a skewer into the egg. If ready, clear juice will appear on the surface. Just before serving top with a mitsuba leaf or snow pea sprouts.

• *Other ingredients you can add to this dish are one or two fresh asparagus spears, cut into 4cm lengths, carrot slices or udon noodles. However, since this is a delicate savoury dish the flavours for the fillings should just filter through the egg custard, not swamp it. Limit the number of fillings to 3 per cup.*

Egg Soup Tamago-sūpu

卵スープ

Serves 2

CHICKEN STOCK
approx. 500g [1lb2oz]
chicken bones
2 litres [3½pt] water

1 teaspoon mirin
1 teaspoon light colour soy sauce
1 teaspoon salt
2 eggs, beaten in a bowl
10 stems enoki mushrooms
4 snow peas, blanched
1 stem spring onion, chopped

1. To make chicken stock, place chicken bones and water in a large saucepan and simmer for 1 hour. Occasionally remove the scum from the surface. Discard the bones and strain the stock. Left-over stock can be stored in the freezer.
2. Warm 4 cups of the chicken stock in a saucepan. Add the mirin, soy sauce and salt.
3. While stirring, pour eggs into the soup and mix gently.
4. Cook for 1 minute stirring occasionally.
5. Add enoki mushrooms and snow peas, and pour soup into individual bowls.
6. Garnish with spring onion.

• *Instant chicken stock can be used instead of homemade stock.*

Tofu

Fresh or dried soy beans are delicious cooked in a variety of ways, but there are also many products in the Japanese diet derived from soy beans. The most common of these are soy sauce, tofu, nattou (fermented beans), soy powder and soy milk. The white bean curd known as tofu appears regularly on Japanese tables. Being a rich protein source, it is a healthy substitute for animal products. Depending on how much liquid is extracted from the curds during the manufacturing process, it becomes silken tofu (kinu-goshi-dōfu) which is quite soft and difficult to handle, or cotton tofu (momen-dōfu) which is much firmer. It is also available as deep fried tofu (abura-age) sold in block form or as pouches used in inari-zushi.

Vacuumed-packed fresh tofu is available from supermarkets everywhere. Once you've opened the packet, refrigerate any leftovers in water in an air-tight container. Change the water every day and the tofu will remain fresh for a couple of days. If you detect a sour smell, discard it.

Before cooking tofu, it is best to extract the liquid from the tofu, unless you are cooking a hot pot. To do this cover over with a piece of muslin cloth or kitchen paper. Remove tofu from packaging and place on the cloth. Fold the edges of cloth over the tofu to wrap it. Press with a weight and stand for 20 minutes or so. In humid or hot weather, refrigerate.

It is often eaten on its own with a dipping sauce or in a miriad of dishes such as miso soup, miso dengaku (grilled tofu), sukiyaki, mizutaki (seafood hot pot).

Hot Pot Tofu Yu-dōfu

湯豆腐

Serves 2

DIPPING SAUCE
4 tablespoons soy sauce
2 tablespoons rice vinegar
2 tablespoons mirin

1 piece dried kelp, cleaned
1 litre water
1 large, approx. 500g [1lb 2oz]
packet of silken tofu, cut into
about 4cm [1¾in] cubes
shichimi (Japanese seven-spice)

CONDIMENTS
1 tablespoon daikon radish
with chilli, grated
1 tablespoon grated fresh ginger
1 spring onion, chopped

1. Combine dipping sauce ingredients in a saucepan and bring to the boil. Cool and pour into individual dipping bowls.
2. In a large heatproof pot, soak kelp for at least 15 minutes, then bring to the boil.
3. Place tofu onto the kelp, cover and bring back to the boil. Add Japanese seven-spice to taste. Serve in the pot with the condiments sprinkled on top and the dipping sauce on the side.

To make daikon with chilli, use a chopstick to make several holes on the cut side of daikon. Insert a whole fresh red chilli into each hole and grate along the cut edge of the daikon to make an attractive red and white garnish.

tofu 93

Chilled Tofu with Topping (Traditional-style)

Hiyayakko 冷奴

Serves 1 only. Increase amounts proportional to number of servings required.

⅛ small packet silken tofu
1 teaspoon fresh grated ginger
¼ spring onion, chopped
a pinch of bonito flakes
soy sauce for serving

1. Place cut tofu onto a plate, top with ginger, spring onion and bonito flakes.
2. Serve with soy sauce.

Chilled Tofu with Topping (Modern-style) Hiyayakko

モダン冷奴

Serves 2 as an entrée

1 tablespoon extra virgin olive oil
1 anchovy, chopped
¼ garlic clove, chopped
1 cherry tomato, rinsed and chopped
1 teaspoon lemon juice
1 teaspoon soy sauce
2 small green salad leaves
⅛ small packet silken tofu

1. Place a non-stick frying pan over a high heat and add a little olive oil. Add anchovy and garlic and stir over moderate heat for 2 minutes. Transfer to a bowl.
2. Add tomato and pour in lemon juice and soy sauce while mixing.
3. Place green salad leaves and tofu in a bowl.
4. Top with anchovy and tomato mixture.

White Tofu Salad Shiro-ae

白和え

Serves 2 as an entrée

¼ small packet of silken tofu
a pinch of roasted white sesame seeds, ground
½ teaspoon caster sugar
⅓ tablespoon light colour soy sauce
1 tablespoon raisins, soaked in water
1 sprig common mint

1. Place a thick sheet of kitchen paper and tofu on a rack on a plate. Put a weight on top and stand for 15–20 minutes. Pat tofu dry with kitchen paper and place into a bowl.
2. Grind sesame seeds in a mortar and pestle.
3. Add tofu and mix in well.
4. Stir in sugar and soy sauce.
5. Add raisins and mix through.
6. Serve in a bowl, with mint as a garnish.

• *Ripe persimmon, pear or mango can be substituted for raisins.*

Deep-fried Tofu Agedashi-dōfu

揚げだし豆腐

Serves 2 (pictured right)

⅓ small packet of silken tofu

SAUCE
½ cup super dashi (page 66)
2 tablespoons soy sauce
1 tablespoon mirin

1 tablespoon grated daikon radish
potato starch for coating
vegetable oil
½ stem of spring onion, cut length-
ways into thin strands

1. Press and drain tofu for 15-20 minutes. Cut into two squares, approx.
   5cm. Pat tofu dry with kitchen paper.
2. Meanwhile, prepare sauce by simmering dashi, soy sauce and mirin in a
   saucepan for 3 minutes.
3. Squeeze grated daikon lightly with hands to remove liquid and set aside.
4. Dip tofu in potato starch and coat on all sides.
5. Place oil in a tempura pan or heavy frying pan and heat to 170° over a
   high heat.
6. Carefully slide tofu into the oil and deep-fry over a medium heat until the
   surface becomes crispy and golden brown. Drain on a rack or kitchen
   paper.
7. Pour sauce into bowls, and add tofu. Top with grated daikon and spring
   onion.

Grilled Tofu Yaki-dōfu

焼き豆腐

Makes 4 pieces

MISO MIXTURE
1 tablespoon mirin
1 tablespoon white miso
1 tablespoon white sesame seeds
sansho (prickly ash) powder or
shichimi (Japanese seven-spice)

1 small packet firm tofu
1 tablespoon mirin, extra
2 small seasoned nori strips

1. Combine all ingredients for miso mixture in a heatproof bowl and warm in
   a microwave oven for 10 seconds before stirring again.
2. Cut tofu into 4 x 7cm [2 ½in] rectangular blocks and pat with kitchen
   paper. Thread onto bamboo skewers.
3. Lay baking paper on a rack. Place skewered tofu on the baking paper.
   Grill under medium heat, turning over until golden brown on both sides.
4. Spread miso mixture over 1 surface of 2 pieces of tofu and grill until lightly scorched.
5. With the remaining tofu, sprinkle with mirin and top with nori sheet; grill
   without burning the nori.

• *Other topping options include peanut butter mixed with a dash of soy
  sauce and blue-vein cheese.*

Vegetables and Herbs

Fresh Japanese vegetables and herbs are gradually becoming available from local producers outside of Japan. It is exciting to see the way in which new produce has been so openly embraced, giving us easy access to the many ingredients required for cooking international dishes outside their countries of origin.

JAPANESE VEGETABLES

DAIKON, WHITE RADISH
There are many varieties, but Aokubi-daikon, white radish with a greenish tinge around the top end is very popular in Japan. Choose radishes which are firm and succulent. If the skin is wrinkled or soft, the radish is not fresh, and may be dry.

EDA-MAME, YOUNG SOY BEANS
Fresh eda-mame are rarely found outside of Japan. However, frozen eda-mame are available all year around from Japanese grocery shops and some Asian shops.

GOBŌ, BURDOCK
Originally introduced from China as a medicine, burdock has become a commonly eaten root vegetable in Japan. It is said that eating this root stimulates the intestines and prevents stomach cancer. It is used in soup, stir-fries, tempura and salads.

HAKUSAI, CHINESE CABBAGE, ELONGATED CABBAGE
Used in hot pot dishes and pickles.

KINOKO, MUSHROOMS
Nowadays, fresh shiitake, enoki and shimeji mushrooms are available in many supermarkets or greengrocers outside of Japan. Dried shiitake mushrooms are very popular. Soaked in water for at least 15 minutes or overnight, the extracted flavours enhance soups and sauces. The dried variety has more flavour and aroma. Enoki mushrooms have slender stems with tiny white caps and are attached together in cluster. They are eaten in soups, hot pots and stews. Shimeji mushrooms also grow in clusters, but they have short, puffy stems and pale grey caps.

KYŪRI, CUCUMBER
Japanese cucumbers are small and thin, about 20cm [8in] long, a bit narrower than a Lebanese cucumber. The skin has small prickles when it is very fresh and the seeds are soft. It is not readily available outside of Japan. Lebanese cucumbers can be used as a substitute.

KABOCHA, JAPANESE PUMPKIN
This relatively small pumpkin has creamy dots on dark green skin. It is good for stews, grills or tempura. To keep pumpkins longer, once cut remove seeds and trim inside using a knife; wrap in plastic film and store in the refrigerator. The flesh of Japanese pumpkins is soft, with a low water content.

NASU, EGGPLANT
The most commonly used variety of eggplant used in Japan is the small bulb-shaped type.

JAPANESE HERBS

There are many Japanese herbs, but they are not common outside of Japan, although mitsuba and shiso are gradually appearing in Japanese groceries and some specialist greengrocers. You may be able to find Japanese herbs in pots at your local nursery.

MITSUBA, JAPANESE WATERCRESS

Literally, mitsuba means the three leaflets that make up the leaf. This herb has a distinctive aroma and is used in soups, blanched in salads, or steamed savoury egg ('Chawan-mushi' pages 84-85). It is rarely eaten raw.

SHISO, JAPANESE BASIL

There are two kinds, green and red. Red leaves are used mostly in colouring for pickles, such as ginger and plums. Dried and salted shiso, called 'yukari', is popular for sprinkling on rice. You may also use it on cold tofu, grilled fish and so forth. Green fresh shiso leaves are much easier to find. They are used as a garnish with sashimi, tempura, or as a topping for cold tofu or cooked rice. Store in refrigerator wrapped with kitchen paper.

SHŌGA, GREEN GINGER

Now a common root vegetable, green ginger is used as as a flavouring in soups, stir-fries with fish and in tea. The grated flesh can be squeezed to produce ginger juice. Pickled ginger is very popular and is made using young green ginger. Unused ginger can be kept in the freezer, and grated directly from the frozen state to produce juice. However, fresh is always the best.

Seaweed Salad Kaiso Sarada

海藻サラダ

Serves 1

1 teaspoon dried kaiso (seaweed), soaked in water
¼ small red onion, sliced and soaked in water

SESAME MISO VINEGAR DRESSING
1 teaspoon light brown miso
1 teaspoon roasted white sesame seeds
1 teaspoon rice vinegar
a pinch of caster sugar

1. Drain kaiso and onion.
2. Combine all the ingredients for dressing in a bowl. Cover with plastic wrap, and heat in the microwave oven for 5 seconds.
3. Mix together.
4. Serve salad with dressing in a bowl.

• *Convenient dried kaiso is available from Japanese grocery shops.*

Tomato with Yukari Tomato Sarada

トマトサラダ

Serves 1

1 small ripe tomato
a few drops of extra virgin olive oil
a pinch of yukari (dried red shiso) flakes

1. Slice tomato, then stack slices to reform tomato shape.
2. Sprinkle with olive oil and yukari.

Asparagus with Miso Asuparagasu-to-sumiso

アスパラガスと酢味噌

Serves 1

3 stems of asparagus
1 tablespoon light brown miso
a pinch salt
a pinch caster sugar
1 teaspoon mirin
1 teaspoon rice vinegar

1. Discard the hard asparagus stems.
2. Cook in salted boiling water for 1 minute. Stand in cold water until cool then drain.
3. Meanwhile, combine miso, salt, sugar, mirin and rice vinegar in a bowl and cover with plastic wrap. Heat in microwave oven for 10 seconds.
4. Dry asparagus with kitchen paper, place on a plate and serve with miso mixture.

Daikon Salad Amazu-daikon

甘酢大根

MARINADE MIXTURE
½ cup rice vinegar
1 tablespoon caster sugar
1 teaspoon mirin

¼ daikon radish, peeled
¼ carrot, sliced
1 small fresh green chilli
and red chilli, chopped

1. Make the marinade by combining all ingredients in a bowl.
2. With slicer or knife, slice daikon radish thinly, and place in the marinade.
3. With vegetable cutter or cookie cutter, cut carrot slices into shapes, and place into the mixture with the chilli.
4. Stand for at least 30 minutes in refrigerator.
5. Remove daikon, carrot and chilli from marinade and arrange on a dish to serve.

Deep-frying

Deep-frying was introduced to Japan from Europe and China in 16th century. Since then, the method and ingredients have been adapted to meet Japanese ways, finally developing into tempura as we know it today. In a strange turn of events, tempura now travels back to the world it came from, and beyond.

The styles of deep-frying at home are divided into three categories: kara-age, lightly coated with flour or potato flour, tempura, coated with tempura flour and furai, coated with breadcrumbs.

Deep-fried Eggplant Nasu-no-karaage

Serves 2

なすのから揚げ

1 tablespoon mayonnaise
½ teaspoon wasabi paste
1 tablespoon mayonnaise, extra
1 teaspoon light brown miso
3 baby eggplants
3 tablespoons potato starch for coating
vegetable oil for deep-frying

1. To make wasabi mayonnaise, mix mayonnaise and wasabi in a bowl.
2. To make miso mayonnaise, mix mayonnaise with miso paste in a bowl.
3. Cut bottoms off eggplants so they will stand up. With a vegetable peeler, shave off the top layer of skin in stripes down the length of the eggplants. With a sharp knife make several incisions through the thickness of the eggplant to allow for more even cooking.
4. Coat with potato starch, patting in with hands.
5. Heat up oil in a heavy pan to approx. 170°C.
6. Deep-fry eggplants until the skin colour changes to bright purple.
7. Drain on a rack or kitchen paper.
8. Serve with mayonnaise.

Tempura with King Prawns and Vegetables Tempura

天ぷら

Serves 1

TEMPURA BATTER
1 cup tempura mix flour
1 cup cold water

3 green king prawns, deveined
5 carrot sticks
1 slice pumpkin
1 shiso (Japanese basil) leaf
1 seasoned small nori sheet
(6cm x 2cm)

vegetable oil for deep frying
1 tablespoon sesame oil

potato starch or extra tempura
flour for coating

DIPPING SAUCE
½ cup super dashi (page 66)
1 tablespoon soy sauce

1 tablespoon grated daikon
½ teaspoon grated ginger

1. To make tempura batter mix, place flour in a bowl. Add refrigerated cold water. Using a pair of chopsticks or fork gently combine.
2. To prepare prawns, remove the head and shell without cutting off the tail. With a small knife, make a slice from the belly side to open like a butterfly.
3. Prepare oil in a deep pan and heat to about 180°C.
4. Coat prawns and vegetables with potato starch.
5. To check the temperature, drop a small amount of the tempura batter into the oil, and when it quickly floats up, it is ready. Holding one ingredient with tongs, carefully slide it into the oil.
6. Turn over when it becomes light golden colour, and remove when cooked on both sides.
7. Drain on paper towel.
8. Repeat with other ingredients. With thin ingredients like nori or shiso leaves, fry quickly.
9. Serve with tempura dipping sauce (made by mixing ingredients together) and a side dish of grated daikon topped with ginger.

- *Tempura is best eaten just after cooking, so when you are making tempura, have the rest of the meal ready and the table set so that tempura is the last thing you cook before eating.*
- *Tempura can be eaten as a dish on its own, with rice, in dishes such as tendon (page 28).*
- *If you are unable to obtain tempura flour, make a batter using 1 cup plain flour, 1 beaten egg and 1 cup cold water.*
- *Always coat tempura ingredients in potato starch before dipping into the batter.*

Deep-fried Skewered Beef and Vegetables
Kushi-age 串揚げ

Makes 3 skewers

6 cubes lean rump beef
3 small fresh green chillies, seeded,
or green capsicum, cut into
bite-sized pieces
½ small onion, cut into 3
(do not separate layers)
3 quail eggs

1 cup plain flour
1 egg, beaten
3 cups dry breadcrumbs (Japanese
breadcrumbs, if available, are
slightly coarser than Western ones.)

DIPPING SAUCE
English mustard
tonkatsu sauce, available in Japanese
or Asian grocery shops

SAVOURY MAYONNAISE
1 boiled egg, mashed
1 pickled gherkin, finely chopped
parsley, chopped
1 tablespoon mayonnaise

lemon wedges

bamboo skewers

1. Skewer first 4 ingredients onto bamboo sticks.
2. Coat the skewers with flour and dip into beaten egg. Place into the breadcrumbs and coat evenly.
3. Heat up the oil as for tempura (page 110).
4. Deep fry until golden brown and drain on kitchen paper.
5. Serve with dipping sauce, savoury mayonnaise and lemon wedges.
6. To make savoury mayonnaise, combine boiled egg, gherkin and parsley with mayonnaise.

• *Optional ingredients include oysters, cheese (such as camembert or brie), asparagus, fresh shiitake, eggplant, onion, pumpkin or garlic.*

Japanese-style Pork Cutlet Tonkatsu

Serves 4

トンカツ

In Japan, tonkatsu is eaten with oyako-don (page 26), Japanese curry, spaghetti or sandwiches.

4 pieces pork loin (approx.
150g [9oz] each)
a pinch of salt
a pinch of cracked black pepper
1 cup flour
2 eggs, beaten
3 cups coarse breadcrumbs
6 cabbage leaves, sliced
and soaked in water
4 baby tomatoes, sliced
snow pea sprouts
tonkatsu sauce for serving, available
from Japanese grocery shops

1. Salt and pepper the pork. Along the fat, make a few slits with a knife to prevent pork shrinking when deep-frying.
2. Coat pork with flour.
3. Beat the eggs in a bowl and dip in the pork.
4. Remove from the egg and place onto the breadcrumbs.
5. Coat pork evenly with the breadcrumbs, pressing firmly with the hand.
6. Heat the oil to 180°C.
7. Deep fry pork until golden brown. Drain well.
8. Place some sliced cabbage, tomato slices and snow peas on a plate.
9. Serve with tonkatsu-sauce.

• *Since most Japanese food is eaten with chopsticks, when serving larger cuts of meat such as pork loin, slice into bite-sized pieces before serving.*

Savoury Deep-fried Chicken Tatsuta-age

Serves 2

竜田揚げ

200g [7oz] chicken thighs,
cut into cubes

MARINADE
2 tablespoons soy sauce
1 tablespoon honey or caster sugar
1 teaspoon crushed garlic
1 teaspoon grated fresh ginger

2 tablespoons potato starch
vegetable oil for deep-frying

1 Marinate chicken cubes in the soy sauce, honey, crushed garlic and ginger and put in refrigerator for at least 30 minutes.
2. Remove chicken from the marinade; drain and coat with potato starch.
3. Heat up the oil to about 180°C.
4. Deep fry chicken cubes for 1 minute, take out and set aside for 1 minute on a tray.
5. Deep-fry chicken again for two minutes.
6. Drain well on kitchen paper.

• *This tasty chicken is just as good served cold, and is perfect for lunch boxes or a picnic.*

Japanese Croquettes Korokke

コロッケ

There are many varieties of Japanese croquettes, such as crab meat, curry and cheese. They are delicious served cold on sandwiches.

5 new potatoes, peeled
1 brown onion, peeled and minced
vegetable oil
200g [7oz] minced beef
1 teaspoon salt
a pinch of cracked black pepper
2 eggs
2 cups flour
4 cups breadcrumbs

garden salad
tonkatsu sauce for serving, available
from Japanese grocery shops

1. Cook potato until soft and drain.
2. Meanwhile, fry onion in small amount of oil until golden brown, stirring continuously. Add minced beef while stirring and season with salt and pepper. Stir until cooked through.
3. Mash potato with a potato masher in a bowl. Add onion and beef, and combine well.
4. Take about two tablespoons of this mixture in the palm of your hand and make a ball. Flatten and make into little oval shapes. (They can be left as round balls if you prefer, but oval shapes are traditional.)
5. Beat eggs in a bowl and place flour and breadcrumbs on separate plates.
6. With hands, pat flour around croquettes.
7. Dip into the egg and coat with flour; dip into egg again and then into breadcrumbs.
8. Repeat with all croquettes.
9. Heat up the oil in a heavy pan.
10. Deep fry croquettes. When they are golden brown on the outside, remove from the oil and drain well.
11. Serve with salad and tonkatsu sauce.

Teppanyaki—
Japanese Style Barbecue

Teppanyaki is an informal method of cooking food on a portable cook-top or hotplate at the table. 'Teppan' literally means a metal plate or hotplate, and 'yaki' means to grill, roast or barbecue, so the word refers only to the style of cooking, and not the ingredients. There are a myriad of recipes, and you can use an electric frying pan or an outside barbecue as well. Such dishes as gyoza (page 130), okonomi-yaki (pages132-133), yaki-soba (page 80), grilled o-nigiri (rice balls, page 20) can be cooked on a hotplate too. Teppanyaki is enjoyable with alcoholic drinks such as sake, beer or white wine.

Unlike the dramatic performance of the Teppanyaki restaurants, the preparation, cooking and eating of teppanyaki at home is an easy and simple procedure. It is good for small parties, either indoors or out-doors, and suitable ingredients include bite-size pieces of chicken, beef, pork, liver, quail eggs, spring onions, mushrooms, small green peppers, and so forth, which can be cooked singly or threaded onto skewers.

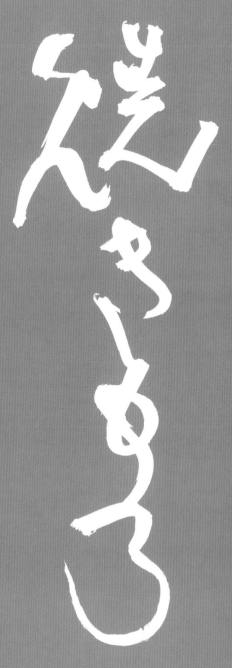

Teriyaki Salmon Teriyaki

Serves 2

テリヤキサーモン

TERIYAKI SAUCE
1 cup super dashi (page 66)
½ cup soy sauce
2 tablespoons caster sugar
1 tablespoon mirin
1 tablespoon fresh ginger juice
(made by grating fresh ginger and
squeezing over a bowl)
1 tablespoon sake

vegetable oil
2 small salmon pieces
a few green salad leaves

Teriyaki sauce is available from Japanese or Asian groceries or major
supermarkets, but you can make your own.
1. To make teriyaki sauce, add all the ingredients in a saucepan and bring
quickly to the boil, reduce heat and simmer for 15 minutes.
2. Drop a little oil onto the base of the frying pan and swirl to coat.
3. Place salmon in the pan, fry over moderate heat for one minute each side.
Add teriyaki sauce and cook 5 minutes over a low heat.
4. Serve in individual dishes, garnished with salad leaves.

- *Instead of salmon, tuna, beef or chicken can be used.*
- *Try marinating ingredients in teriyaki sauce before wrapping with foil
and cooking on the barbecue.*

Pork with Ginger Soy Sauce Shoga-yaki

Serves 2

しょうが焼き

1 cup teriyaki sauce (see page 122)
200g [7oz] sliced lean pork
1 teaspoon ginger juice (made
by grating fresh ginger and
squeezing over a bowl)
vegetable oil
1 garlic glove, crushed
½ brown onion, sliced
and soaked in water
2 cabbage leaves, sliced
and soaked in water

1. Prepare teriyaki sauce. Marinate pork in teriyaki sauce and ginger juice
for 30 minutes.
2. Pour a little oil in the non-stick frying pan and stir-fry onion and pork for 5
minutes or until cooked.
3. Add sauce and cook another minute and serve with sliced cabbage on a
plate.

Salt-grilled Shellfish Shioyaki
塩焼き

1 tablespoon sake (or mirin)
2 green king prawns (push a bamboo skewer through each prawn lengthwise to straighten it prior to grilling)
2 fresh oysters
2 cockles
1 tablespoon salt
2 tablespoons grated daikon
ponzu dipping sauce (page 142)
2 lemon wedges
1 tablespoon chopped chives

1. Sprinkle sake over the shellfish.
2. Sprinkle salt on top.
3. Over medium heat, grill both sides of seafood.
4. Serve with grated daikon, ponzu dipping sauce and lemon wedges. Garnish with chopped chives.

• *Small fish such as yellow tail or whiting can be used instead of the shellfish*

Barbecued Chicken Yakitori
焼き鳥

Makes 8 skewers

Yakitori is skewered chicken, flavoured with sauce or salt, grilled over a charcoal fire. In specialised small shops throughout Japan known as Yakitori-ya, barbecued titbits of chicken meat, livers, hearts, intestines and skin are served with alcohol. Yakitori-ya are always crowded with people on their way home after work.

1 cup teriyaki sauce (page 122)
200g [7oz] chicken thigh fillets cut into bite-sized cubes
8 chicken livers
8 chicken giblets
3 spring onion stems, cut into 3cm [1¼in] lengths
8 Japanese green peppers (or any colour capsicum), seeded and cut into bite-sized pieces

bamboo skewers

1. Make teriyaki sauce.
2. Thread chicken ingredients, peppers and spring onion onto bamboo skewers.
3. Cook skewers in a frying pan, grill under the griller, or barbecue on the open grill or hibachi (Japanese griller), turning often and occasionally brushing with sauce.

Home-style Teppanyaki Yaki-niku

Serves 4

焼肉

YAKINIKU SAUCE
1 cup super dashi (page 66)
1 cup soy sauce
1 whole garlic, peeled and grated
1 apple, peeled and grated
¼ cup roasted sesame seeds
¼ cup rock sugar (koori-zatou),
available at Asian supermarkets
¼ cup sake
¼ cup mirin
2 tablespoons honey

4 small eggplants or
1 large eggplant, trimmed
400g [14oz] beef brisket, sliced
1 carrot, peeled and sliced
2 onions, sliced
1 red capsicum, seeded and sliced
1 green capsicum, seeded and sliced
1 corncob, cut in quarters
4 thin slices Japanese pumpkin

Japanese mayonnaise

vegetable oil

1. To prepare yakiniku sauce, combine all the ingredients in a saucepan and bring to the boil. Simmer 20 minutes over low heat. Allow to stand with lid on until cool. You can store this sauce in a refrigerator for 2 weeks.
2. Slice eggplants lengthwise and place in salted water for 10 minutes. Rinse and dry with clean kitchen paper.
3. Prepare beef and other vegetables and place on a large plate. Put sauce and Japanese mayonnaise in small dishes.
4. Use either electric pan or a portable stove and frying pan to cook at the table.
5. Heat pan, add a small amount of oil and invite each person to start cooking their own selection, using chopsticks to lift the pieces in and out of the pan.
6. Dip in sauce or mayonnaise before eating.

Dumplings Gyōza

ギョーザ

DIPPING SAUCE
½ cup soy sauce
⅓ cup rice vinegar
1 teaspoon sesame oil
1 teaspoon chilli oil

DUMPLING MIXTURE
60g [2½oz] minced pork or king prawn
¼ teaspoon chopped garlic
1 teaspoon grated ginger
1 Chinese cabbage leaf, chopped
5 stems Chinese garlic chives (nira), chopped
a pinch of salt

10 round gyōza or gow gee wrappers

vegetable oil

¼ cup water

1. To prepare dipping sauce, mix all the ingredients in a bowl.
2. Place all the dumpling fillings in a bowl and combine well.
3. Place a wrapper on a dry plate or board and, using one finger, wet round the edges.
4. Put 1 tablespoonful of filling on the centre of the wrapper.
5. Fold the wrapper over the filling, seal the edges together by pressing and making small pleats. Repeat with remaining wrappers.
6. Heat a non-stick frying pan and add a little oil, swirling around the pan.
7. Lay a few gyōza side by side in one or two rows in the pan (depending on size of pan), and cook on one side until golden brown. Then using a spatula, turn over 1 row all at once (so as to avoid breaking the dumplings). Add water and put a lid on to steam. Steam for a couple of minutes or until most of the liquid has evaporated.
8. Serve hot with dipping sauce.

• *Gyōza dipping sauce is available from Japanese grocery shops.*

Savoury Japanese Pancake Okonomi-yaki
お好み焼き

Makes 1

Okonomi means 'of your choice' or 'as you like it' so include ingredients of your choice along with egg, flour and cabbage as the basic ingredients.

OKONOMI-YAKI SAUCE
2 tablespoons Worcestershire sauce
2 tablespoons tomato sauce
1 tablespoon soy sauce
1 teaspoon caster sugar

50g [2oz] self raising flour
¼ cup milk
¼ cup super dashi (page 66)
a pinch of salt
1 egg
1 spring onion stem, chopped
1 cup thinly chopped cabbage
2 king prawns or thinly sliced pork or cuttlefish

aonori (green-seaweed) flakes for topping
dried bonito flakes for topping

Japanese mayonnaise

1. To make okonomi-yaki sauce, mix ingredients together in a bowl.
2. Place flour, milk, super dashi and salt in a bowl and lightly stir.
3. Break an egg into the mixture and stir to combine.
4. Add spring onion and cabbage and mix.
5. Heat a non-stick frying pan over moderate heat, swirl oil over base of pan.
6. Drop the egg mixture into the pan. Top with king prawns.
7. Cook until bubbles appear on the surface. Turn over and cook for about 4–5 minutes occasionally flattening with a spatula, until cooked through.
8. Brush the top with okonomi-yaki sauce, and sprinkle aonori and bonito flakes on top.
9. Serve with Japanese mayonnaise.

* *Cheese and chicken can also be used in this dish instead of seafood or meat.*
* *Okonomi-yaki sauce is also available from Japanese grocery shops.*

Stews and Hot Pots

Nabe is the Japanese word for pan or pot, so nabe-mono probably equates to the Western casserole, though the cooking methods may be different. Nabe-mono are usually cooked on a portable burner, or in an electric pot or frying pan at the table, with everyone sitting around, serving themselves from the pot, adding in extra ingredients and supervising the cooking. In some ways, it is rather like the European fondue style of cooking. It is a most pleasant way to warm up in winter. Soy sauce and dashi are the predominant flavourings, often with a touch of sweetness. It is a simple way of cooking. Meat or seafood and vegetables are cut up beforehand, and cooked in a dashi mixture which is simmering in a pot on the table. If a portable burner is not available, the meal can be cooked in a pot on a regular stove and brought to the table, which is just as tasty, but of course does not create quite the same cosy atmosphere.

Nabe are usually served with a side dish of steamed rice. Sake makes a good accompaniment, as does dry white wine.

Beef and Vegetable Stew Niku-jaga

Serves 2

肉じゃが

1 new potato, cut into small pieces
vegetable oil
200g [7oz] finely sliced brisket beef
or oyster blade (Finely sliced beef
is available from Asian butchers
or Japanese groceries.)
1 small onion, peeled and sliced
1 carrot, peeled and cut into pieces
½ packet shirataki noodles (gelatinous noodles) or rice noodles
¼ cup caster sugar
2 tablespoons mirin
2 cups water
2 cups super dashi (page 66)
4 tablespoons soy sauce
6 snow peas, trimmed

rice balls (page 20)

1. Trim corners of potato to avoid breaking when cooking.
2. Pour a little oil in a saucepan and swirl over the base.
3. Add beef, onion, potato, carrot and shirataki noodles; stir for a couple of minutes.
4. Add sugar and mirin; stir again.
5. Pour water and dashi into the pot. Cook for 15 minutes, occasionally removing the scum from the surface.
6. Add soy sauce and snow peas and simmer with a lid on for a further 15 minutes.
7. Serve with rice balls or a bowl of steamed rice.

Sukiyaki

すき焼き

Serves 4

There are regional differences in the preparation of sukiyaki. In the Tokyo area, sukiyaki sauce mixture (warishita) is made beforehand, whereas in the Osaka area, the sugar, mirin, soy sauce and dashi are added during cooking. Cooking is always done at the table.

600g [1lb5oz] Scotch fillet or sirloin fillet, finely sliced (slicing the fillet half-frozen makes it easier)
1 large packet momen (firm) tofu, cut into small cubes
1 carrot, cut in julienne slices
8 fresh or dried and soaked shiitake
1 bunch edible chrysanthemum leaves (available from Asian grocery stores)
4 spring onion stems, cut diagonally
¼ Chinese cabbage
1 packet harusame noodles or udon noodles cooked and drained
4 eggs
vegetable oil

SUKIYAKI SAUCE
⅓ cup caster sugar
3 tablespoons mirin
⅓ cup soy sauce
500g super dashi (page 66)

steamed rice, as accompaniment

1. Prepare meat, vegetables and noodles and place on a plate.
2. Break eggs into individual bowls and beat lightly.
3. Make sauce by combining all ingredients.
4. Set a portable cooking plate or electric frying pan on the table and heat.
5. Oil the pan, and start cooking by sautéing the spring onion, then add some of the beef, followed by small portions of the other ingredients and the sukiyaki sauce, a little at a time. Make a space for further ingredients by pushing the cooked ones to one side with chopsticks.
6. As the food cooks, guests can serve themselves by dipping the hot food into the beaten raw egg and eating with a bowl of rice.

• *When the pot has been cooking for some time, the taste will become quite concentrated. At this stage, instead of adding sukiyaki sauce, water or a little sake can be added.*
• *Other ingredients such as enoki or shimeji mushrooms can be included.*

Shabu-shabu

シャブシャブ

Shabu-shabu is a word which cannot be translated directly, but it represents the sound made by the slices of meat as they are swished around the pot when dipped in the stock, rather like the lapping of water on the side of a boat. Traditionally, this dish would be served at home with a side dish of steamed rice.

500g [1lb2oz] thinly sliced sirloin beef (available frozen from Asian butchers or Japanese groceries.)
500ml [¾pt] water
a sheet of kombu (dried kelp), approx. 5 x 10cm
¼ Chinese cabbage leaves cut into bite-sized pieces
1 packet enoki mushroom, stems dicarded
1 small packet silken tofu, cut into cubes
1 packet fresh shiitake (or 8 dried shiitake, soaked)
1 packet harusame noodles, cooked according to directions on packet
1 bunch edible chrysanthemum leaves (available from Asian and Japanese grocery shops)

1 x 5cm [1¾in] length of peeled daikon, with red chilli inserted through slits, then grated

1. Soak kombu in water in a large saucepan or casserole dish (kombu-dashi, page 65).
2. Prepare the meat and vegetables and arrange on a large plate.
3. Heat water and kombu dashi in a pot on a portable cook top or electric frying pan on the table. Bring to the boil with lid on. When boiling, remove the kelp.
4. Family and guests sit around the pot and start cooking. Keep stock simmering continually. Using chopsticks, add beef, cooking until it just changes colour. Add vegetables to the pot, a little at a time.
5. Remove portions from the stock, dip into sauces (page 142) and eat with daikon.

Goma-dare (white sesame seeds) Dipping Sauce

胡麻ダレ

3 tablespoons sesame paste (or substitute tahini),
1 tablespoon sake
4 tablespoons caster sugar
1 teaspoon soy sauce
4 tablespoons roughly ground white sesame seeds

1. Combine sesame paste, sake and sugar in a bowl and stir until well mixed.
2. Add soy sauce and sesame seeds and mix in well.

Ponzu Dipping Sauce

ポン酢

½ cup light soy sauce
½ cup lemon or lime juice
⅓ cup rice vinegar
1 tablespoon tamari soy sauce
3 tablespoons mirin
1 x 5cm kelp sheet, finely shredded

1. Combine all the ingredients. Allow sauce to stand overnight.

Vinegar-soy Sauce   su-jōyu

酢醤油

½ cup soy sauce
½ cup rice vinegar
1 teaspoon mirin

1. Combine all ingredients.

Homemade Light-tasting Soy Sauce

ホームメイド・ライト醤油

1 cup soy sauce
2 cups super dashi (page 66)
1 tablespoon sake
1 tablespoon mirin

1. Combine all ingredients.
2. Bring to boil, and simmer for 5 minutes. Store in a capped bottle in the refrigerator for 1 month.

Seafood Hot Pot Mizutaki

Serves 4

水炊き

1 litre kelp dashi (page 64)
2 snapper fillets, cut into bite-sized pieces (for filleting see page 52)
a pinch of salt
4 scallops in shells
8 green king prawns
8 cockles
8 dried shiitake, soaked
1 bunch edible chrysanthemum leaves
¼ Chinese cabbage
1 packet harusame noodles or rice noodles, cooked and drained

1 cup goma-dare (white sesame seeds), vinegar-soy sauce (su-jyōyu) or ponzu dipping sauce (page 142)
½ cup grated daikon radish

1. Heat kelp dashi in a large casserole dish or saucepan.
2. Place snapper in a bowl and rub with salt. Stand for 5 minutes.
3. Prepare other ingredients and place on a large plate. Put dipping sauce into individual bowls. Place daikon radish in a bowl. Set them on the table.
4. Set portable stove or electric pan on the table.
5. Put kelp dashi in the pot and simmer.
6. Add some of the snapper fillets and other ingredients and simmer. Discard any scum which may float to the surface.
7. Diners can serve themselves, using chopsticks, and dipping food into the sauce. Add more ingredients to the pot as the contents get low.
8. Serve accompanied by dipping sauces and daikon.

Drinks and Desserts

Although coffee, teas and soft drinks are widespread in Japan, drinking green tea at meals is still part of Japanese life. In this chapter, I introduce Japanese green teas, cold drinks and desserts combining Western techniques with Japanese flavours. They are simple and easy to make.

After Japanese green tea leaves are picked, they are steamed. Depending on the time of the year, the picking period, type of leaf and processing, the natures of the teas vary greatly.

Here are some common Japanese teas:

Sen-cha
This is the green tea drunk most commonly in the home Make tea with water slightly below boiling, 80-90°C to reduce bitterness.

Hōji-cha
Roasted 'Ban-cha' green tea. It has slightly larger leaves than 'Sen-cha' green tea, and a roasted rice aroma. It contains less tannin and caffeine compared to other green teas. If green tea has become old and flavourless, it can be reborn as hōji-cha by roasting in a dry (non-oiled) pan.

Mugi-cha
Roasted barley tea. It is drunk cold as a summer drink. It is often sold in packs which make one litre.

Mattcha
Powdered green tea which is drunk at special occasions, such as a tea ceremony. It is also used in Japanese confectionery, ice-cream, and so on. It is very bitter, so it is traditional that it be served with a small Japanese sweet.

Cold Barley Tea and Cold Sweet Ginger Juice
Mugi-cha and Hiyashi-ame 麦茶と冷やし飴

Ginger juice is refreshing after a summer swim or as a warm drink in winter.

a packet of mugi-cha
(barley tea) tea bags
1 litre [1¾pt] water, boiling
extra 750ml [1¼pt] water
100g [4oz] palm sugar or rock sugar
1 tablespoon honey
5cm [1¾in] knob of
fresh ginger, sliced
1 teaspoon grated ginger

1. Place tea bag in a heatproof pot and pour in the boiling water. Leave to cool, discard the tea bag, and refrigerate. (You can store this tea in the refrigerator for 1 week.)
2. Make sweet ginger juice by bringing the extra water to the boil in a saucepan. Add palm sugar and honey, and stir gently until dissolved.
3. Place ginger slices and grated ginger in the saucepan, simmer for 20 minutes, occasionally stirring.
4. Remove pan from the heat and allow mixture to cool. (You can store this in a refrigerator for 5–7days.) Before serving, strain.

Soy Milk Jelly with Black Sugar Glaze
Gyūnyū-kan 牛乳カン

Serves 4

½ cup black sugar
¼ cup water
200ml [⅓pt] water
4g agar agar powder (available
from Asian grocery shops)
2 tablespoons caster sugar
400ml [⅔pt] soy milk (without sugar)
4 cherries for garnish

1. To make black sugar sauce, place black sugar and ¼ cup water in a saucepan, and simmer for 3 minutes. Cool.
2. Place extra water and agar agar powder in a saucepan, and combine well.
3. Bring mixture to the boil, continuously stirring. Simmer for 2 minutes.
4. Add caster sugar and stir until dissolved.
5. Remove from the heat, add warmed soy milk and mix well.
6. Pour into a flat-based container and refrigerate until firm.
7. With cookie cutters, cut into star-shapes or simply slice. Serve on a plate, glazed with black sugar or decorated as you wish.

• *Cut into star shapes, this makes an attractive Christmas-season dessert. Japanese people love to celebrate festivals, and although Christmas is not a traditional festival, these days it is becoming embraced by the Japanese as another reason to party.*

Soba Cookies Soba Bōro

蕎麦ボーロ

80g [3oz] soba wheat, ground,
available from health food shops
100g [4oz] plain flour
1 teaspoon baking powder
1 egg
80g [3oz] caster sugar
extra flour

1. Preheat oven to 180°C.
2. Sieve together soba wheat, flour and baking powder.
3. Beat egg in a bowl. Add sugar and whisk to combine well.
4. Add flour mix and stir with a spatula.
5. Transfer the mixture onto a sheet of baking paper, sprinkle with a little extra flour and knead lightly.
6. Wrap in plastic wrap and refrigerate for 30 minutes.
7. Roll out the dough between sheets of non-stick baking paper until 5mm [¼in] thick. Cut the dough into shapes using cookie cutters.
8. Place on baking trays lined with non-stick baking paper. Bake for 13–15 minutes at 180°C until lightly coloured.

Ginger Sherbet Shōga-shābetto

しょうがシャーベット

Serves 4

1 tablespoon grated ginger
150g [5oz] caster sugar
1 cup water
2 egg whites
1 teaspoon gin (or rum)
finely grated lime zest and mint
for garnish

1. Place ginger, caster sugar and water into a saucepan over high heat. Stir until the sugar has dissolved, and simmer for 5 minutes. Remove from the heat and set aside to cool.
2. Put the egg whites into a bowl and beat with a whisk until soft peaks form. Add cooled ginger mixture and gin, then stir to combine.
3. Transfer to a container, cover and set in the freezer for approx. 4 hours. Every 30 minutes, stir with a fork and return to the freezer.
4. Serve in glasses topped with finely grated lime zest and mint leaves.

Sake Granita Kachiwari-sake gōri

かちわり酒氷

Serves 4)

½ cup water
1 cup sake
½ caster sugar

1. Place water, sake and caster sugar in a saucepan over high heat. Stir until the sugar has dissolved. Remove from the heat. Allow to cool.
2. Transfer the mixture into an ice cube tray. When frozen, put the ice cubes in a plastic bag, wrap with a towel and break up with cooking hammer into crystals.
3. Serve as for ginger sherbet.

Green Tea Cake Ocha-no-kēki

Makes 1 loaf-shaped cake

お茶のケーキ

3 teaspoons green tea leaves
40g plain flour
45g cornstarch
¼ teaspoon baking powder
3 eggs, separated
80g [3oz] caster sugar
a pinch of salt
icing sugar
mattcha (green tea) powder

1. Line a 10cm x 20cm loaf tin with non-stick baking paper.
2. Grind tea leaves finely using a mortar and pestle.
3. Sieve flour, cornstarch and baking powder together in a bowl. Set aside.
4. Place egg yolks and sugar in a bowl and beat with a whisk. Place the bowl over a saucepan of water approx. 70°C and whisk until the mixture becomes creamy white. Remove from the water. Continue to whisk for 3 minutes or until cool.
5. Whisk egg whites and sugar in a bowl until soft peaks form.
6. Add ¼ egg white to the egg yolk mixture and combine with a spatula. Add sieved flour and combine.
7. Add remaining egg white and tea leaves and fold in without breaking the form of the white.
8. Transfer mixture into the loaf tin. Place in pre-heated oven (160-170°C) and bake for 30-40 minutes.
9. When cooked, allow to cool and, using a small sieve, dust half the cake with icing sugar and half with the mattcha powder.

INDEX